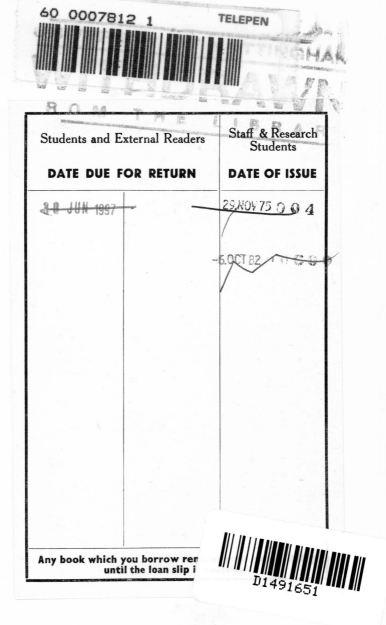

THE SLATE FIGURES
OF CORNWALL

By

A. C. BIZLEY

(Alice C. Butler, R.M.S.)

with a Foreword by

DOROTHY DUDLEY, M.A., F.S.A.

Alice C Bizley

The publication of this book has been assisted by a grant from the Marc Fitch Fund

Printed by
WORDEN PRINTERS
MARAZION AND PENZANCE

" *It is only by these fragments that remain, and sometimes when one looks upon their memorials in the quiet Cornish churches, the seasons racing by outside the windows, that one has a sudden apprehension of these men and women long dead and of what they were when they were alive, going about the countryside on their concerns. In those moments, it is as if one were listening to the beating of their hearts, and they all the more intimate and moving, being dead.*"

A. L. ROWSE.
" Sir Richard Grenville of the Revenge."

ACKNOWLEDGMENTS

I am very grateful to my friend Miss Dudley for her Foreword and for giving me ready access to her library. Also to Dr. A. L. Rowse for his practical and kind encouragement and for allowing me to use an extract from his book, *Sir Richard Grenville.*

During the preparation of this record, I have received a lot of help from many people, to all of whom I am most grateful. Especially I would like to thank Mr. H. L. Douch, Curator of the Royal Institution of Cornwall, who first suggested I should attempt this study, and for giving me so much encouragement and guidance; the Federation of Old Cornwall Societies and the Hon. Secretary, Mr. L. R. Moir, for the gift of several line blocks and some very useful advice; and Mr. P. Hull for his patience and help in research at the Cornwall County Record Office.

I would also like to express my appreciation for the assistance I have received from the Rev. Dr. R. G. L. Beazeley, Miss B. Spooner, Mrs. Evelyn Mann and Major Christopher Morshead; also my thanks to the Royal Cornwall Polytechnic Society for the gift of a line block, Mr. J. Setchell of the Old Delabole Slate Co. Ltd., the Rev. A. R. Lintell and the Rev. Roger Ellis.

To many Old Cornwall Societies who have given me continuous and active support; those people all over the County who have kindly allowed me to look at their houses; my daughter for her work on the typescript and my husband for his constant and enthusiastic help, I am most grateful.

Finally, I would like to express my warmest thanks to Miss P. M. Angove for having read and improved my manuscript and to Messrs. Worden Printers Ltd., for their understanding co-operation.

ALICE C. BIZLEY

September 1965

St. Annes
  Tywarnhayle Road
    Perranporth

CONTENTS

ILLUSTRATIONS

FOREWORD

CORNISH churches retain a very strong regional character and lovers of these ancient buildings will feel grateful to Mrs. Bizley for directing attention to the Slate Memorial Slabs in both Church and churchyard. These unique monuments are a speciality of Cornwall and this is the first book to describe and delineate them for, until now, they have been strangely ignored.

Our Churches are storehouses of treasures from the Past and both interest and appreciation grow where there is expert guidance to their meaning and history. With years of hard work in church and library, the authoress has interpreted these memorials to us in a knowledgeable and sympathetic way. She has traced the development of the making of these monuments and shewn them to be the work of local craftsmen from the fifteenth to the eighteenth centuries: in some instances she has been able to find the name of the workman.

Many memorials are costly affairs of excellent workmanship and reveal a story of some greater family; they recall to us the old saying— "Their desire is in the work of their hands." Others are poorer monuments to lesser people and are generally by a less-skilled hand; some are badly treated and some neglected. Yet all possess an individuality and seem to touch truly on life and death; fragments of the craftsman's humour, too, are displayed—" changeless yet never stale."

Mrs. Bizley points out our responsibility for the preservation of these monuments and, also, towards the many slate headstones existing in our churchyards; these frequently exhibit fine carving and beautiful lettering but are often seen shifted from their rightful place to a meaningless row elsewhere. Here is another theme demanding research and that quickly; can we hope that Mrs. Bizley will again deserve our warmest thanks and rescue these " frail memorials " from an undeserved oblivion.

DOROTHY DUDLEY.

INTRODUCTION

IT is not surprising to find gravestones of slate inside most of the churches and in every churchyard in the diocese. For slate, or Cornish marble as it is sometimes called, is a very durable stone, plentiful and easily worked and it has been quarried and widely used throughout Cornwall for more than four centuries. The gentry and merchants of Elizabethan Cornwall found it the ideal material, at a moderate cost, for putting up family monuments which would satisfy their vanity and impress their neighbours. It also encouraged the yeoman families to indulge their own fancies or to copy the style set by the gentry.

Many of the early monuments bear the figures of men and women boldly carved in relief. Those which have survived the hazards of time remain as unique examples of a Cornish craft and they are remarked upon by Mr. Sacheverall Sitwell in his introduction to *English Church Monuments* by the late Katharine Esdaile. He says, " Such another group of local monuments to be enjoyed in a particular district, and nowhere else, is represented in the Elizabethan slate reliefs in Cornwall, as at St. Tudy, with kneeling figures and much lead-cistern decoration, the whole constituting something rare and peculiar to that far county outside or beyond England."[1]

As long ago as 1881, E. H. W. Dunkin listed and described the engraved brasses of the county in his book *The Monumental Brasses of Cornwall*; yet no complete record has ever been made of the tombs and panels of slate with effigies of the deceased carved upon them. This seeming neglect of such interesting examples of local art may, in part, be explained by the difficulties of recording these very sombre and sometimes dilapidated sculptures.

It is seldom possible to obtain a satisfactory rubbing, certainly not from the relief carvings and the incised specimens are usually too roughened to admit of a clear outline. Photographs can be very helpful in some degree, but the simple line drawing has proved to be the most successful method of reproduction.

In this book a careful record has been made of every slate carved with the figures of deceased men and their families. Sixty-four still remain in forty-seven of the parish churches of Cornwall; and one in the churchyard at St. Enodoc. Some notes have also been included concerning a few decorated panels and headstones which are of particular interest.

---

[1] Esdaile, p. 32. This may be making too big a claim, for there are a few similar memorials in Devon; they could have been the work of Cornish carvers but, as they are unsigned, there is no certainty.

1

Nine monuments have been preserved intact and they each consist of a tomb-chest and backplate. The kneeling figures of the deceased man and his family were usually carved upon the backplate, or panel, and fixed to the wall behind the tomb: a single figure was carved and set horizontally on the top of the chest. The front and end panels of the chest were decorated with armorial bearings or additional family figures and patterns.

Many of the figured panels which have been recorded can be recognised as remnants of similar monuments and by observing the arrangement of the border inscription or design, their original position can be understood.

The majority of the carved figures are in the north and east of the county and there are some near Looe: in the west only at four churches, Madron, Ludgvan, Lelant and Lamorran. They date from 1500 to 1727; the earliest example is the floor-slab bearing the figure of Humfrey Calwodely at Helland and the latest date, 1727, is on the memorial to Sarah Cottell at Kilkhampton. The craft was evidently at its peak between 1575 and 1650 as most of the slate panels recorded are in that period. A number of them are probably of Delabole slate, famous for its fine texture and enduring qualities, but some local quarries, long since worked out would also have provided slate of varying quality and colour.

The old carvers first cut their figures in high relief, and those at St. Tudy (1575—1597) are three very fine specimens; but quite soon they began to forsake such a difficult style to work in low or shallow relief, and finally to use the incised line, no doubt finding it better for drawing in detail and at the same time reducing the risk of flaking.[2] It is impossible to define more exactly the periods to which these different styles of carving belong as the figures which have survived can only be regarded as a part of the original number produced.[3]

Some of the early carvings were fully coloured but such embellishment seems to have lessened along with the depth of carving and was hardly used at all on the incised effigies.

As one would expect, the best materials and carvers were employed by the more important and well-to-do families; whereas the smaller gentry and the yeomen ordered slate from the nearest quarries to be carved by the local masons. It is this wide range of quality in both material and workmanship which makes the study of these slate monuments so fascinating, especially those cut and fashioned by local men. These worked as individualists rather than from a stylised pattern as used by professional carvers or sculptors. What art these men lacked in being able to produce a realistic figure is more than compensated for in the many delightful and often appealing details of dress or design.

[2] E. Brown, E. Everard, *The Architectural Review*, Vol. XCV,
[3] Jago, J.R.I.C. No. XXII, p. xxxiii—iv,

For example, the man who carved the slate in Morval church (1634) was able, with the help of the then much favoured vine decoration, to draw only the two small figures of Walter Coode and his wife (she in a simple widow's wimple) and to represent each of their eight children by a bunch of grapes. But although some of these rural craftsmen may have found the proportions of the human body rather beyond their powers of drawing, they were often capable of executing some good and attractive lettering. The simple slate commemorating Jane Merifeld (1662) at Michaelstow shows a gallant attempt by one carver to put rather more into his lettering than he had in his drawing. It will be noticed on some of the more crudely cut slates how the carvers were occasionally obliged to add a letter or word which, being unable to read, they had left out of the inscription. A particular example of this is on the Kempe slate (1624) at Blisland.

The early memorials, those between 1575 and 1598, carved in bold relief, are all by professional carvers and of these the splendid and complete tomb of John Bevill at Talland (1578) is one of the best. This is a fine example of the craft of Peter Crocker, one of the few carvers whose names remain cut on their slates. The recumbent figure of Philip Mayowe too (1590) at St. Martin-by-Looe should be accepted as his work for although there is no signature on the re-constructed monument, there is a close similarity to that of the Bevill tomb, in the drawing of the hair and moustache, the covering of both armour and robe with elaborate patterns, and the figures each set deep within their fine border inscriptions. He also carved the coffin-shaped panels of Margery Budockshide at Lansallos (1578) and Ann Smith at Duloe (1592), while at Pelynt there is yet another of his robustly carved figures, the likeness of William Achym (1589).

It is possible that Crocker produced some of the other remaining monuments of that early period, such as the magnificent coloured panels of the Vyell family at St. Breock (1598) and the Wrey tomb (1597) now at Tawstock. At least there can be no doubt that the Vyell slate and the Wrey tomb were carved by the same man whoever he was.

The Hechins panel at St. Stephen-by-Saltash (1593) although very similar in style is of coarser workmanship and rather suggests a poorer craftsman copying a traditional pattern. The remaining three panels belonging to this early period are those of the Nicoll and Reskymer families at St. Tudy (1598—1575). These carvings are outstanding as they are magnificently cut in such bold relief that the praying hands project from the body. Except for some flaking on the Nicoll panels, these three slates are in exceptionally fine condition, due perhaps in some measure to the " protective " covering of blacklead with which they were heavily coated for many years until carefully cleaned by a late rector of St. Tudy, the Revd. J. C. Nankivell, M.A.

Another carver to sign his work was Anthony Colly in 1634 on a slate panel to Cordelia Trelawney at Pelynt; and in 1666 on the very large and splendid panel to John and Catherine Verman at Lamorran. This monument has certain features in common with the large unknown slate at Duloe which may also be the work of Colly.

A very fine slate with the incised figure of Peter Bolt (1633) at Bodmin and another equally well cut slab showing Richard Courtney (1632), only three miles away at Lanivet, share a similar technique in the life-like drawing of the face and may therefore have each been carved by the same hand.

Four other slabs which are obviously the work of one particular carver can be seen at Stoke Climsland (Mannington 1605), Lezant (Trefusis 1606), Northill (Vincent 1606) and Bodmin (Durant 1608). On each of these slates the style is the same, the mask-like faces of the kneeling figures and the shoe heels of the women showing below the hem of their gowns.

There are no other memorials sufficiently alike to be able either to pair or group them until the very late examples carved in the 18th century classical style by Michael Chuke at Kilkhampton and Poughill in 1727 and 1723.

The pattern books issued in the sixteenth and seventeenth centuries by booksellers in the Low Countries were largely bought by provincial sculptors of this country; and also the Books of Emblems, " in which everything in heaven and earth was illustrated and twisted to convey a moral, obvious or the reverse." The clumsy and ugly designs in these early books were in time improved and the crude compositions with kneeling figures found in the Rhineland and southern Sweden were made symmetrical and pleasing and the kneeling figures flanking a prayer desk became the typical English monument for seventy years.[4]

This style of monument has been used for all the large Cornish family slates, which tends to rob them of the naive charm to be found in the humbler carvings. So in a similar way the verses and symbolical devices on the professionally carved slates have not the original freshness of the homespun rhymes. One delightful example is on the Kempe slate at Blisland (1624) with its eight lines of verse extolling the virtues and advantages of marriage and parenthood; another is the Tanner slate at St. Enoder (1634) giving words of quaint comfort for the loss of a young wife and mother. Some more verses on the family memorial at Mevagissey (1632) make very descriptive and entertaining " play " on the name of Dart.

It is interesting to find on some of the simpler slabs, curious and unexpected details, as on the slate carved with the figures of John and Alice Mably (1687) in the churchyard at St. Enodoc. Either because of inexperience or having an original turn of mind, this carver embellished the capital letters of the inscription with tiny faces! Incidentally the Mably tomb is unique in being the only one of the " figured " slates of Cornwall to be found *in situ* in the churchyard. There is a panel at

4 Esdaile, p. 91.

Werrington from a dismantled monument but it is fixed to the outside wall of the church. Unfortunately nearly three hundred years of exposure to the weather has left its mark on the Mably slate, which (besides being broken and rudely joined with iron staples) has become so covered with lichen as to be hardly legible. It is a great pity that so little care has been taken of such a delightful specimen of an ancient craft.

According to the custom of the 16th and 17th centuries, the figures of whole families, father, mother and children, were often carved on a monument which commemorated only the death of the father; even grandchildren were sometimes included as at St. Cleer on the Langford tomb (1614) where nine grandchildren are shown; and there are ten grandchildren on the panel of Thomas and Alice Cock and Thomas Fleming at Madron (1631).

Children were dressed very much like their elders and it is particularly interesting to see how the carvers tried to indicate their ages. Very young girls are sometimes shown wearing bonnets tied under the chin instead of a hat or head-dress like their mothers. The small slates of Mary Verman at Lamorran (1668) and Elizabeth Pollamounter at St. Columb Minor (1640) are examples of this. Then at Mevagissey the three youngest boys of the Dart family have no hair on their faces or cushions to kneel upon, like their father and elder brothers. With girls the order of seniority is usually shown by the amount of pattern or trimming on their gowns, as well as the number of kneeling-cushions. On two panels there are the full length figures of infant boys wearing gowns with hanging sleeves; these occur at St. Enoder on the Tanner slate and on the Bennet slate (1630) at St. Teath. Except for the hanging sleeves and uncovered heads these little boys look very like their sisters. The most appealing of all the children, however, is the incised carving of the baby boy in his mother's arms at Talland (1634). This slate is beautifully cut and full of heartwarming detail.

In the south aisle of Northill church among the Spoure monuments there is a fragment of slate on which is incised a curious little figure wrapped in a cloth, rather like a pudding! This rough drawing represents a chrisom child. A chrisom was the white robe put on a child at baptism by the priest after he had anointed it with chrism.[5] If the child died within the month after baptism it was customary to wrap it in its chrisom for burial. There are two other carvings of chrisom infants: one with the large Durant family at Bodmin and the other on the Tanner slate at St. Enoder.

Fashions changed slowly in the country and this would have been especially true of so remote a county as Cornwall in the period covered by these memorials. As a result the Elizabethan style of dress still persisted on slabs as late as 1636, at Ludgvan.

With two exceptions, all the men on the early slates wear armour and sometimes two swords and, of course, their Elizabethan ruffs. The

[5] Consecrated oil.

wives too, match their impressive husbands in their elaborately patterned gowns, gold chains and girdles and dignified head-dresses. From a passing glance, the patterns on the gowns appear to be all alike, but upon closer inspection it will be seen that although following the same basic design they each have their own individual details.

Only two ladies of this early period wear high-crowned felt hats. They can be seen in the carvings of Margery Budockshide at Lansallos and Ann Smith at Duloe. These two women were sisters-in-law, which may explain the close similarity of their monuments. The head-dresses referred to were a kind of Tudor bonnet with the addition of a wide piece of material extending from the middle of the forehead and back over the head to hang loose to the shoulders. But as none of the carvings are in profile, one cannot be sure if there is a drape such as belonged to the traditional hood. This unusual attachment has not been observed on any paintings or sculpture contemporary with the Cornish slate carvings and it may well have been a style peculiar to the married gentlewomen of Cornwall.

In spite of the slow change of fashion there is a good variety of costume to be enjoyed among the monuments carved from 1600 onwards when the figures of other people, such as priests and yeomen, were also carved on slate.

The five effigies of priests which remain provide a wide range of dress beginning with Lewis Adams (1609) at St. Breward, dressed as a layman in tunic and breeches and fur-trimmed coat; then William Cotton (1611) at Minster wearing a flowing gown and skull cap; and John Bagwell (1623) at Stoke Climsland, a curious little figure in a plain jacket and breeches. John South (1636) at Ludgvan wears a long straight robe with hanging sleeves and Laurence Braginton (1723) at Poughill is in a loose robe and close fitting cap.

The smallest of the slate carvings are the four delicately incised little tablets attached to John Hender's stone memorial (1611) at Minster representing each of his four daughters with their respective husbands. The technique of these carvings and the style of dress shown are very like those of the engraved monumental brasses. Two slate tablets seen at Monkleigh in Devon are similarly engraved and could be by the same craftsman.

The amount of information collected of the personal history and background of the families in this record of slate memorials is sometimes very small. Some were yeomen and so did not bear arms; others were small gentry who led uneventful lives in remote villages; and again, quite a number of wills and inventories of the Bishop's Court which can be so rewarding for other counties, were destroyed in the bombing of Exeter during the 1939—45 war. Yet, in spite of all, this study of Cornish families has shown very clearly what an insulated community they were, seldom marrying outside their own county. Richard Carew in 1602 remarked on this custom: " This angle which so shutteth them in, hath wrought many interchangeable matches with each other's stock, and given beginning to the proverb, ' that all Cornish gentlemen are cousins '."[6] An example of how closely knit they could become occurs with Ann Smith (carved at Duloe) who, by her second marriage, became aunt to one of her own daughters! As for their actual dwelling places, these, where they still exist, have been visited but being of secondary importance to the subject of this book they are not described in any detail.

Contemporary with the 17th century " figured " slates are some very fine heraldic and decorated panels. Some examples carved with armorial bearings can be seen at Crowan (Godolphin 1652), Sithney (Arundell 1671), St. Columb (Arundell 1701—1752) and St. Enoder (Tanner 1747). The decorated panels are elaborately carved with designs of fruit, flowers, angels heads and emblems of mortality; especially noteworthy designs can be found at Blisland (Toker 1686), St. Eval (Leach 1687) and Cubert (Lawrence 1699). The decorated ledger stone commemorating Perran Hosken (1671) at Perranzabuloe is illustrated as representative of a similar style of memorial which continued after the carved figures had gone out of fashion.

The slate panels remained in favour through the eighteenth century, when the carving of angels became so popular on headstones and on the slate ledgers covering the tombs of brick and stone in the churchyards. These 18th century angels present a versatile and entertaining company; some of them are delicately drawn, ethereal creatures; some would easily qualify as imps with their fat little bodies and spindly legs and some quite definitely belong to the avenging angel class. An early and unique example of an angel in flight is preserved on a floorslab to the memory of Humphrey Pethick (1663) at Week St. Mary.

It cannot be claimed that the Cornish slate carvings, even the best of them, have any great sculptural merit. Many of them are clumsy, out of proportion and crude; but they will always draw the attention of anyone who is interested in detail. These carved slate memorials deserve more than a passing glance, for unless one is prepared to give then an unhurried and careful inspection, many of the curious and unexpected details mentioned in the text will be missed. Nothing is superfluous, whether it is the stitching to distinguish a blanket, or a bell to denote a bell-founder.

The patterns of the women's gowns have already been described, so alike but each having a subtle distinction. Many other delightful designs have also been used in a variety of ways, to decorate cushions, borders and backgrounds. It would be a very rewarding task to collect and record these ancient patterns and perhaps perpetuate some of them in the adornment of our present-day furnishings.

The heraldry shown on the slates is another detail worthy of close study, for it can so often supply family information not otherwise known,

[6] Carew, p. 64.

or which has been wrongly recorded. Although mistakes in spelling occur, through the illiteracy of the carvers, the family arms are always reliable as they had to be checked by the Heralds.[7]

A number of the monuments are not in their original positions and those which were formerly in the chancel were evidently moved during the various church restorations as the place for monuments came to be re-assessed. Others have obviously spent many years outside and these were either victims of the Civil War years when the churches were stripped of so much of their furnishings; or of subsequent restoration work.[8] St. Columb Minor church which was bare of monuments in 1882[9] now has some very interesting examples, mainly of slate, probably brought inside during the restoration of 1889. At St. Ervan a similar restoration has had compassion on more than a dozen quaintly carved panels.

Only one panel of figures remains outside and that is stapled to the wall of the church at Werrington.[10] Considering that the present church was built as late as 1742, one wonders why such an interesting memorial was not preserved inside the building.

During fifteen years of studying and drawing the memorials, it has been most encouraging to find these often unnoticed carvings being appreciated and in some places re-sited and cleaned. The incumbents of the parishes concerned in this record have been very helpful in giving their consent for drawings to be made and photographs taken and sometimes in tracking down elusive family details.

A further and most important work waiting to be done is the recording of the slate headstones of the 18th and 19th centuries. The need is urgent, for the growing tide of enthusiasm to make a clean sweep of old headstones from our churchyards, threatens to engulf these simple stones with their delightful carvings and lettering—long since out of fashion but not out of mind.

[7] A particular example of this occurs on the slate panel to Mary Arundell at Duloe, where the arms shown are those of Arundell impaling Cary. In the Arundell pedigree (as given in *Vivians' Visitations of Cornwall*, p. 12). Thomas Arundell, the father of Mary, married Mary Capell daughter of Sir Gamaliel Capell. He did in fact marry Julian, the eldest daughter of George Cary Esq., of Clovelly and his elder brother, Sir John Arundell of Trerice married Mary the second daughter of George Cary. *Visitations D*. p. 157.
[8] J. C. Cox, *County Churches, Cornwall*, 1912, p. 44.
[9] A. J. Jewers.
[10] See p. 169.

ST. ALLEN

John Marten 1626

Position: Forming the sill of a window in the north aisle.

Size: Across the top 4 feet 4 inches, the bottom 5 feet 6 inches and depth 2 feet 1 inch.

Condition: Good.

Style: A border inscription with corner designs of an acorn, rose, thistle and a stylised flower, is set round a cartouche containing a verse with an elaborate pattern of rose and thistle set on either side. Good lettering and interesting capitals.

Inscription: Hic Jacet sepultis Johannes
Marten Junior de Trefronick
qui obijt tertio die Maij Ano Domi 1626.
May'st, dost, or raust thou feare,
My gentle freiend
To view the goale, where to mankind doth tend
From to earth, must earth returne againe
Either by accident or lingring paine:
The only way to sollace thee in death,
Is to be confident in him whose breath,
Whose bloud expird was shedd to ransome all
To heavenly ioyes from hell's eternall thrall.

Trefronick remains as a farm in St. Allen about one mile north from the church and, although the old house can still be recognised, it is now reduced, possibly in size, and certainly in character.

The following short inventory of 1626 remains:[1]—

The Inventorye of all the Goods and Chattles moveable and immoveable of John Marten of Treronecke in the pishe of St. Allen lately deceassed valued and praised by Richard Steven and Hannibal Lobb XXVIth. daie of June 1626 in manner and forme ffollowinge

Imprimis his purse, girdle and wearinge apparrell price *iiijli*

Itm one cuppboard, one square table 2 Board one deske and a coffer *xxiiijs*

Itm in Bookes	*lxs*
Itm in Wooll	*xljs vid*

Itm one Saddle, one bridle and other trifflinge things *vjsiiijd*

Itm an estate of one close of Lande in the Borough Town of Michell for Trme of *iij* yeeres and *vii* monethes, from the tyme of his death *vli vijs vjd*

Itm *xxij* sheepe and *ij* Lambs *iiijli vs*

Suma totalis 17-13-4

[1] C.R.O.

9

ST. BLAZEY

Digory Tonkin 1701

Arms: Or, a chevron gules between 2 Cornish choughs in chief and a cannon in base, mounted on a carriage, sable.

Position: On the north wall, close to the organ.

Size: 6 feet by 2 feet 9 inches.

Condition: Fine surface and in excellent condition.

Style: Carved in relief and set within a border of a coiled leaf design is a shield showing the arms of Tonkin. Below it is a figure of Time, bearded, winged, and draped, carrying an hour-glass in his left hand and a sickle in the right hand. Above the head a skull and " Memento Mori " and below the feet " Resurget " and crossbones.

Inscription: Here lyeth the body of Digory Tonkin
Merchant of this Parish who
departed this life the 17th day of
February Anno Domi 1701
in the 34th year of his age.

BLISLAND

Humfry Kempe 1624

(Plate 1)

Arms: Gules, three garbs Or.

Position: On the north wall of the Sacrament Chapel.

Size: 6 feet by 2 feet 8 inches.

Condition: Some flaking across top left corner otherwise good. Rather soft light grey slate.

Style: Of crude design and lettering. The figures, cut in low relief, are of Humfry Kempe kneeling with two sons and facing them across a prayer stool with book is Jane his wife, and two daughters. Above the figures is a shield displaying the arms of Kempe impaling Peyton. Attached to the back of the mother is a skull signifying the death at birth of the firstborn daughter Radigan. Beneath the figures is set out a quaint and philosophical verse.

The surrounding border inscription is so arranged as to be easily read, which suggests that this slate was never intended as the cover for a tomb-chest.

Inscription: Heere Lyeth the Body of Humfry, sonne and Heyre
to Thomas Kempe of Lavethan Esquire Who departed this
Life the Tenth Daye of November Anno Domi 1624 and
Married Jane the Daughter of Thomas Peytonne Esquire
Customer of Plymouth Cornwall.

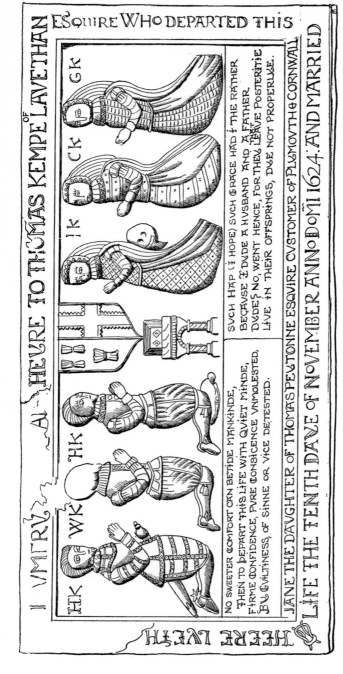

Plate 1

BLISLAND
Humfry Kempe 1624

No sweeter Comfort can betide mankinde,
Then to Depart this Life with quiet minde,
Firm Confidence, pure consicence unmolested,
By Guiltiness, of sinne or vice detested.

Such hap (I hope) such grace had I the rather
Because I dyde a husband and a Father,
Dyde? No, went hence, for they that leave Posteritie
Live in their offsprings, dye not properlye.

The family of Kempe settled at Lavethan about 1500 following the marriage of William Kempe with Grace, daughter of John Boscawen of Tregothnan.

His great-great grandson Humfry, to whom the slate is dedicated, married Jane, daughter of Thomas Peyton customs officer of Plymouth and Cicely, daughter of John Bourchier Earl of Bath.

In the bottom left-hand corner of the slate there is carved the Bourchier knot which was the badge of that family.

Of the other figures on the slate, William, the eldest son survived his father by only five years and his brother Humfry died three years later in 1632.

William's son William sold Lavethan in 1654 and removed to Veryan. This senior line ended in three co-heiresses.[1]

Lavethan is delightfully situated about half a mile west from the church.

Susanna Toker 1686

Arms: Azure, eight Barrulets wavy Argent, over all on a chevron embattled counter embattled Or between 3 sea horses naiant of the last, 5 gutte de pois.

Position: Attached to wall behind the pulpit.

Size: 5 feet by 2 feet 8 inches.

Condition: Perfect.

Style: The inscription is set in an oval framed between two ornamental pilasters and a floral design, with a winged angel's head above. The top portion of the slab is filled with a shield and crest bearing the arms of Toker impaling Mathew, and some strapwork decoration. A handsomely carved slate.

Inscription: Near this place is interred the Body of Susanna the Wife of Christopher Toker of this parish Gent. and daughter of Richard Mathew of St. Kew Gent deceased which departed this life May the 12th In the year of our Lord 1686 Being in the 25th year of her Age.

[1] Maclean, part 1, vol. 1, p. 74.

BODMIN

Jowdy, Katheren and Richard Durant 1589 1608 1632

(Plate 2)

Position: On the wall of the south aisle near the font; formerly attached to the east wall of the D.C.L.I. Chapel, but during 1960 was removed to its present position.

Size: 4 feet 10 inches by 2 feet 5 inches.

Condition: A soft slate which has suffered a certain amount of flaking, but it has now been cleaned and oiled against further deterioration.

Style: The carving and design of this slate is very crude and shows a border inscription beginning with a large capital letter and having a rose cut in the bottom left-hand corner. Within the border are the kneeling figures of Jowdy and Katheren Durant with their families of six and fourteen children and fruitful vine decoration. Above them is a descriptive verse of ten lines. The youngest child is shown wrapped in its chrisom.[1]

> *Inscription:* Here lie ye bodies of Jowdy and Katheren, Wives unto Richard Durant, of this Towne, we departed this life in the faithe of Jesus Christ, Jowdy was buried the 25th of May, 1589: and Katheren the 22nd of December 1608. Here lyith the body of Richard Durant, Husband unto these wives, and father unto these children, twice Maior of this Town, who departed this life in the faith of Jesus Christ, the 20th of May, Anno Domini 1632. Aged 79.

During their lifes, had Durant wifes, Jowdy and Kathren named,
Both feared god & eke his rodd, so well their lifes they framde.
both comly, frugall, chast & fruitfull; yea of a constant mind
to all their friends, even to their ends, still to their husband kinde
both children dear whiles they lived heer unto their husband brought
by him a score they had no more, all in good nurture taught.
The first had 6, 14 ye next, bookes of recorde doe tell
the best is this and trew it is, they livde and died well,
And here doe lie, whose children crie, woe yt this day wee see,
They must be still, it is God's will, they ar gone, and so must wee.

Upon the open book in front of the first wife is written, " Beholde the mercyes of god to his glory " and on her eldest son's book, " Vivo hodie, morior cras. T.D. Sic transit Gloria Mundi." The second wife's book has the inscription " I come Jesus—I lyved to dye & dyed to live againe."

Richard Durant was twice Mayor of Bodmin, in 1611 and 1624.[2] His son Thomas held that office in 1641 and 1653.[3] Richard was first

---

[1] Introduction, p. 5.
[2] Maclean, Pt. I, Vol. I, p. 236.
[3] He was also Reeve of the Manor of Bodmin, Maclean, Pt. I, Vol. I, p. 151.

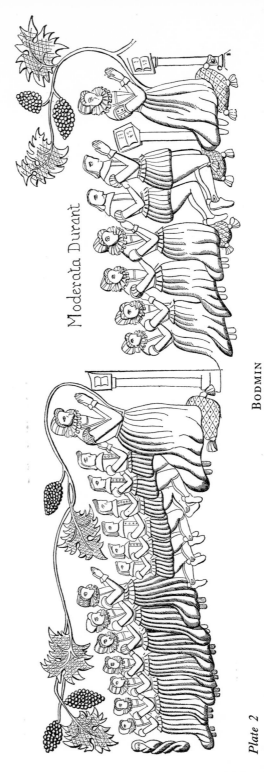

Moderata Durant

BODMIN

Carved figures from Panel to Durant Family 1632

Plate 2

Plate 3   BODMIN
                          Peter Bolt 1633

married on January 7th 1582 to Jowdy Mitchell and in the seven years until she died she bore two sons and four daughters. The second marriage was to Katheren Turny on November 14th 1590 who bore six sons and seven daughters and died in 1608 at the birth of her fourteenth child.

Peter Bolt 1633

(Plate 3)

Position: On the west wall near the font. Formerly in the D.C.L.I. Chapel.

Size: 6 feet by 2 feet 6 inches.

Condition: Excellent. Cleaned and oiled in 1960.

Style: Well cut in low relief by a skilled carver is the full-length figure of Peter Bolt wearing the embriodered fur-trimmed robes of a merchant and holding a book in his left hand. The main inscription is within a border of trailing vine but a label set beside the figure completes the family details. A twelve-lined verse covers the lower half of the figure.

Inscription: Here lieth the body of Mr. Peter Bolt merchant, sometyme steward of ye Citye of Exceter who departed this life in the feare of God, the 26th of July, Ano. Domi. 1633; and also ye body of Elizabeth his daughter, buried ye 14th of April 1628. Which Peter Bolt had 2 wives and 13 children, 5 sonnes and 8 daughters.

> Seaventy six dozen moones and odd
> a Stewardship I held of God.
> of wch when he accompt did call
> pale death me nothinge did appale
> because the judge (severe of late)
> is now become myne advocate;
> who having fully payd and prayd,
> both for my sinnes and savinge ayde,
> (sterne Justice and mild mercy meeting,
> and trueth and peace each other greeting.)
> guided my soul by heavenly love
> to raygne for aye with God above.

Peter Bolt was a member of the Merchant Adventurers Company as shown by the shield of arms cut on the slate. " The ancestor of this family lived at Worsted (Horstead?) in Norfolk about 1500 and was called John. His son Robert, citizen and mercer of London, died in 1533—he is said to have had a grandson named Peter, sometime steward of Exeter afterwards removing to Bodmin— "[4]

⁴ C. S. Gilbert, Vol. II, p. 35.

ST. BREOCK

William & Jane Vyell 1598

(Plate 4)

Arms: Argent, a fesse ragulee Gules between 3 pellets.

Position: Against the west wall of the south transept, or Trevorder Aisle.[1]

Size: 13 feet 8 inches by 6 feet.

Condition: Excellent. A crack near the female figure.

Style: Carved in bold relief, the figure of William Vyell in full armour kneels before a prayer stool on which is a blue cloth with gold fringe and a closed Bible. His wife Jane, in a red brocade gown, kneels behind, and between them are shields bearing the arms of Vyell and Arundell.
They are set within the framework of a traditional scroll design which is supported by the crude figures of Adam and Eve. Above them are displayed twenty shields showing the ancestry of Vyell and Arundell, and surmounting all a combined shield of arms with crests, and the date 1598. Below the two central figures are set six large shields displaying the marriage alliance of each of their daughters. In its present form this slate occupies the wall space almost from floor to roof and would seem to be the backplate and front and top panels of the original tomb-chest. The main inscription in Latin is on the top panel now placed at the foot of the monument and partially concealed by benches.

Inscription: 1598
> Things that b ecciding exelent
> Be not comenli longe permanent
> Veritie Vanquisheth . . . Viell
> William Dennes of Orleighe maried Marie Viell ye Eldest
> Gorge Granville of Penhele maried Juliane ye Second daughter
> Nicholas Predeaux Soldour maried Cheston ye third daughter
> Gorge Arundell of Lanherne maried Dorethe ye Fourth daughter
> Peter Bevill of Blos maried Grace ye Fieffth daughter
> Gillese Risdon of Boblye maried Elizabeth ye sixe daughter.

William Vyell was the son of John Vyell and Isabella Carminow of Trevorder in St. Breock. He married Jane, daughter of Sir John Arundell of Trerice by his first wife Mary, daughter and co-heiress of John Bevill of Gwarnick.[2]

William died February 8th 1590 and his wife on April 21st 1592. In her will dated April 15th 1592,[3] Jane gives " to all and everie of my Servauntes bothe men and women a quarters wages over and above that which is or shalbe due unto them." In addition a number of them

---

[1] Writing in 1882 A. J. Jewers described this slate as Delabole and against the E. Wall of the S. transept.
[2] *Visitations* C., p. 549.
[3] P.C.C.

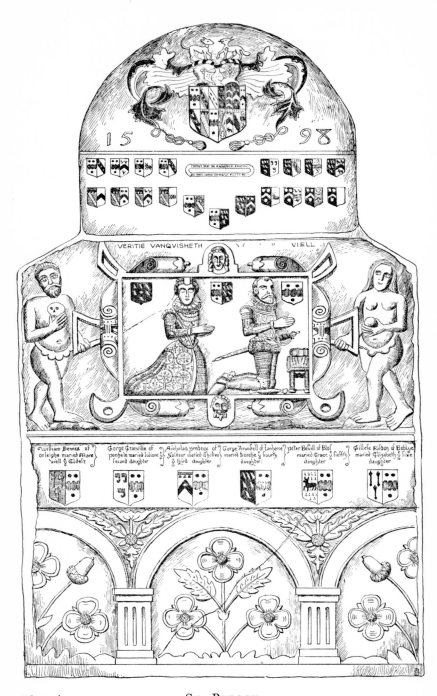

Plate 4　　　　　　　　　ST. BREOCK

The backplate and front Panel from the tomb of William and Jane Vyell 1598

also received gifts of cattle, including " the little boie William and Wilmott the little maide, to either of them a heiffer of twoe yeares olde."

After all her debts and legacies were paid, Jane bequeathed the rest of her property to her six daughters " and the same to be amongst them equally divided, lovinglie and friendlie without anie striffe or contention."

There is an interesting entry from the diary of William Carnsew of Bokelly for January 18th 1577[4]: " Walked about my ground, Mr. Sheriff[5] with me, who rode to William Vyell's to make a marriage for George Grenville with Jill Vyell. 19. Rode to Camelford with the Sheriff; met George Grenville there. 21. At Trevorder; met Mr. Arundell Trerice, Mr. Carew, George Grenville who promised to marry Jill Vyell."

Trevorder, a farm, lies about one and a half miles south-east of the church. The present modern house at Trevorder contains one old room —a small square parlour with its original varnished panelling. This has been painted to resemble marble but one panel has a well executed representation of a classic castle or fortified wall in the manner of Claude Lorraine. The old front doorway of granite is dated 1652 and has a square hoodmould and ornamental spandrels. In the east gable has been inserted a curious little granite light or window with a cusped head—about one foot by six inches.[6]

" Trevorder was the seat of the Billings in the 15th century and was carried to the Viell family by the marriage of George Viell (grandfather of William) with Elizabeth the elder co-heir of Richard Billing. John Viell in 35th Henry VIII was assessed to the subsidy in St. Breoke upon land of the value of 40 marks per annum—a high rate at that time. Trevorder afterwards passed to Sir Nicholas Prideaux of Solden by marriage with Cheston daughter and co-heir of Viell and became the seat of Prideaux in Cornwall."[7]

Charles Tredeneck 1578

Arms: Or, on a bend Sable 3 bucks heads cabossed.

Position: Attached to the south wall of the Lady Chapel.

Size: 6 feet 8 inches by 7 feet 2 inches.

Condition: Good.

Style: Under a semi-circular pediment is displayed a shield of twelve quarterings bearing traces of colour and supported by two boldly carved putti and the date 1578. Below the carving is the inscription divided by an ornamented panel on which is cut at the top " 1578 " and " the XII of Maye " and at the bottom a shield bearing a fess between three female heads.

[4] A. L. Rowse, *Sir Richard Grenville*, 1937, p. 127—129.
[5] Sir Richard Grenville.
[6] Henderson, Vol. III, p. 118.
[7] Maclean, Vol. I, Part II, p. 684.

Inscription: 1578. Gloria, mundi, vitru, est, cum, splendit, frangit,
  qd, C.T.
          Yow chyldren whych on earth remayne,
          Beholde of man the bryttell state:
          Know thys of trewthe, judge all thyngs vayne,
          What in thys woreld dyd God create,
          But that we see ryght every daye:
          Eche thynge to change and passe away.
          Yea, man, I saye, most perfecte wrought,
          Whom God created pryncypall.
          Doth he not quyckely turne to nowght:
          When God agayne hys spyryte doth call,
          Then all hys thowghtts perysshe ech on.
          Nothynge on earthe can comforte than.
          Loe, where hys body dothe nowe lye.
          Whose lyfe of late was helds so deare,
          Well worthye of good memorye.
          Thow happye Charelse Tredeneck, esquire:
          Whose vertuse, yf they had byn knowen.
          Were many mo' then erste were showen.
          Know yow therefore deathe taryeth not:
          and how the covenante of the grave
          Ys showed to us for flesshe ye wote,
          No powre nor strength of all can have:
          ffor when departs awaye hys breathe
          He turns agayne unto hys earthe.
          Do good therefore, whyles you have lyfe:
          Holde vertue of the cheffeste pryse.
          In wysedomes lore be alwayes ryfe:
          These are the counsels of the wyse:
          Depende not then on thyngs most vayne,
          Nothinge but vertue shall remayne.
          Charles Tredeneck was the eldest son of John and Frances Tredeneck
of Tredeneck. He married Elizabeth daughter of Thomas Marrow of
Warwickshire and had five sons and eight daughters, of whom one son
and two daughters predeceased him.[8]
          In his will[9] he desired to be buried " without any worldly pomp . . .
that my debts be paid with as much spede as conveniently they maye."
To each of his surviving and unmarried daughters, Prudence, Elizabeth,
Florence, Katheryn and Honour, he bequeathed a hundred pounds to
be paid unto them at the age of twenty-four years " or before if their
mother do so think good." To each of his three younger sons Dudley,
Robert and Weldon, he gave eight pounds yearly to be paid out of his
lands and tenements in the Barton of Pawton, " when they should
accomplish the age of twenty four years."

[8] *Visitiations C.*, p. 558.
[9] P.C.C.

" To Elizabeth my wellbeloved wief whom I make my sole executrix
. . . all my lands tenements goods and chattels, the lease of the Barton
within the Lordship of Pawton wch I lately bought of one Trubelfield . . .
and all such lands as my late uncle William Tredenecke of Cardinam
gave unto me . . . if my wief doe marrye that then she shall leave the
house at Tredenecke to my sonne (Francis aged 13 at his father's death)
Well furnished wth all the lands to the same And she to have twenty-
three pounds yearly paid unto her by my heire."

The final bequest " to Elizabeth Cruse my kynswoman and servant
mayden six pounds thirteen shillings fourepence at her marrieage."

Tredeneck is sited on high ground about a quarter of a mile west of
the church. No trace of the house remains among the present-day farm
buildings.

ST. BREWARD

Lewis Adams 1607

(*Plate 5*)

Position: On the north wall of the chancel.

Size: 4 feet by 2 feet 5 inches.

Condition: Good except for some broken edges.

Style: Carved in low relief, the man kneels before a prayer stool upon
which is a cloth and a closed Bible. He wears a fur-trimmed gown with
hanging sleeve, over his doublet, His wife, in a high-crowned hat and
full-skirted gown, kneels behind him. The surrounding border has
flaked away at each end so that only part of the inscription and trace of
decoration remains. Carved on the slate beside the figure of the woman
are the words, " This worke was made at the cost of John Adams his
sonne 1609."

Inscription: Lewis Adams departed this Lyfe the XXIII day of
August in Ano dom 1607. Vicar of Breward XXXIII yeres and
so ended this lyfe.

J. Adams
The Godly life hee lived
Hee to the worlde dyd showe,
But heere remains his bed
tyll sounde of Trumpe shall blowe;
Let children learne by this my cost and payne
not to let dye, ther buried Father's fame.

A small slate tablet measuring 2 feet 7 inches square is fixed on the
wall beside the larger slab. It consists of a decorated border with
arched top and in the top corners are the crudely cut letters E and A.[1]

[1] Commemorates John, the son of Lewis, at the top is the name J. Adams, and on the corner
of the slab L. A. (his widow's initials) Maclean, Pt. I, Vol. I, p. 373.

St. Breward
Lewis Adams 1607

Plate 5

A Terrier for St. Breward of approximately 1604 is preserved[2] bearing the signature of Lewis Adams as follows:
A note concerninge the vicaradge of Breward.
Imprimis. the vicaradge is gyven by the Dene and Chapter of the House of Exone.
Item. there is about XXX ackers of Lande belonginge to the Gleebe of the said vicaradge and is bounded in the Estate weste northe with the landes of the lordes of the maner of Hametethy and on the south with the comons of the seid maner.
Item. ther are no implementtes belonginge to the said vicaradge
Item. the valuacion is eight powndes.

Christopher Rogers 1604
(Plate 6)

Arms: Argent, a chevron between three bucks trippant Sable, differenced with a mullet.

Position: In the south-east corner of the south aisle.

Size: 5 feet by 2 feet 6 inches.

Condition: Poor.

Style: Carved in low relief, the man kneels on a cushion before a prayer stool upon which is a closed Bible. He wears a sword attached to the belt of his doublet. Behind him kneels his wife wearing a thimble-crowned hat above her ruff and full-skirted dress. This slate is in very poor condition with much of the detail worn away, including the border inscription. Between the figures there remains some trace of lettering and the date 1609.

Inscription: Christopher Rogers, gentleman, who deceassed this life the XV day of May, in the yeare of our Lord God one thousand, six hundred, and foure. This worke was made to the cost of Reginald Rogers, gentleman, 1609.[3]

This slate and the one commemorating Lewis Adams were probably the work of the same carver.

Christopher was the eldest son of John Rogers and descended from a family of that name who settled in Bodmin at an early date. A John Rogers who contributed to the rebuilding of Bodmin Church in 1470 is described as of Lanke in St. Breward. Christopher married Mary, daughter of William Langdon of Langdon in Jacobstow and they had one son Reginald who married Richarda, daughter of Richard Crossman of Lancarffe, and two daughters, Elizabeth the wife of Hugh Wills of Helland, and Ann the wife of Robert Robins of Blisland. Reginald was the last male descendant of his family, his only son Richard, dying in infancy.

Lanke, a well preserved farm, lies about a mile and a half south of the church.

[2] C.R.O.
[3] Lake, Vol. I, p. 143.

St. Breward
Christopher Rogers 1609

1609

Plate 6

Nicholas Burrough 1654

Arms: A chevron between three fleur-de-lis.

Position: Fixed to a stone at floor level on the north side of the south aisle.

Size: 4 feet 8 inches by 2 feet.

Condition: Fair. Bottom right-hand corner broken, obliterating words.

Style: Within a border inscription is a quaint paraphrase of Psalm 131 and some lines from Act II Scene VII in Shakespeare's "As you like it." Some simple drawings of vine and flowers fill the remaining spaces between the words.

> *Inscription:* Here lieth the body of Nicholas Borrough Gentleman
> who was buried the . . . o Domi 1654[4]   Psalm 131
> The world is like a play where every age concluds his scene
> (and) so departs (the) stage. Thus . . . playes post . . . his
> naturs . . . forgeting . . . and takes it for . . .
> O Lord I am not puft in mind
> I have no scornful eye
> I do not exercise my selfe
> in things that be to hye
> But as the child that weaned is
> even from his mothers breast
> so have I Lord behaved my selfe
> in silence and in rest.

Nicholas Burrough of Penquite had five sons and one daughter. In the churchyard there is a tomb bearing the arms of Burrough and commemorating John, grandson of Nicholas and his wife Beatrice and son John dated 1712.

Penquite is situated about three quarters of a mile south of the church on high ground above the village. The original house is now a ruin with a modern farmplace built around it and known as Higher Penquite.

The remains of the old house consist of two ground-floor rooms which form one side of a small enclosed courtyard; the other side is now a barn with drip stones visible above blocked window spaces. Other interesting details include a stone fireplace, a small arched granite porch on the south side, another low arched granite doorway into the courtyard, and near it a small mullioned window and a stone carved with the date 1618.

---

[4] Nicholas Burrough, buried 13th March 1654. St. Breward Par., Register.

c

William Billing 1654

Arms: Or, on a bend Sable, three bucks heads erased of the first, a crescent for difference.

Position: Set against the east wall of the south aisle.

Size: 3 feet 6 inches by 4 feet 3 inches.

Condition: Good.

Style: The top of the slate is ornamented with a border of strapwork and a small centre arch under which are incised the arms of Billing. Below this are set the inscription and verse in a plain border between two pilasters of fanciful design.

> *Inscription:* William Billing of Lanke gent. was buried the 17th
> day of February 1654.
> > A character of the deceased shal be
> > No subject of this strait epitomie;
> > Expect no large encomiums at al,
> > No thing of stern now panegyricall
> > Charnels and Tombs need only hint but this,
> > Survivor, heed thy metamorphosis.

William was the eldest son of Reginald Billing and nephew of Richard Billing of Hengar in St. Tudy. He married Johanna, daughter of— Stilston and had four sons and seven daughters. His eldest son Richard died in 1660 leaving an infant son who did not reach maturity. The estate of Great Lanke passed to his younger son John Billing.

Great Lanke was parcel of the possessions of the family of Hocken. Upon the marriage in 1592 of Reginald Billing, second son of William Billing of Hengar and Ann daughter and heiress of Thomas Hocken, it was conveyed to the Billing family. In 1627 Reginald Billing rebuilt the house, as is shown by the remains of two arched granite doorways still remaining.[5] The smallest of these two doorways was, and still is, the main entrance to the house, the other being the entrance to the courtyard. A fragment of the embattled courtyard wall remains in the garden with the head of an ancient cross. At the base of the modern garden gate is a block of granite inscribed R.B.1627.

The house and lands passed from the Billing family in 1813 and was later altered and in part rebuilt. Great Lanke now has a very plain and dilapidated appearance but retains some splendid outbuildings with arched granite doorways.

---

⁵ Maclean, Vol. I, p. 381.

CALLINGTON

Ann Holliday 1753

(Plate 7)

Position: Fixed to the outside wall of the south porch.

Size: 4 feet by 2 feet 10 inches.

Condition: Excellent. A light green slate of fine texture.

Style: Carved at the top in low relief is an oval, framing the figures of three angels; two in flight with trumpets and holding back a drape, while a smaller angel bearing a cross and banner stands triumphantly on the skeleton of death. Underneath is the inscription, set between fluted and decorated pilasters, followed by an epitaph. At the bottom, inside a circle, is the figure of a woman wearing a long loose robe and a veil. She kneels on a cushion before a desk which has an open book and a lighted candle upon it. Inscribed around the design are the words " Watch and Pray "; and the name John Burt Callington Sculp: At each corner of the slate is carved a charming angel's head.

Inscription: Here Underneath Lyeth
the Body of Ann ye Daugh-
ter of James Holliday
and Joan his Wife of this
Borough who Departed this
Life the 23rd Day of July 1753
Aetatis Suae 28
O cruel Tyrant Death that could not spare:
A sober lovely Girl that was so rare:
In gifts of nature and in grace Divine
Amongst us for a time did brightly shine.
She that in pious paths so even trod:
Is Enoch like, translated to her GOD:
Who by her Death did evidently show
Lov'd her too well to leave her here below.

Plate 7   CALLINGTON
Carved figure from the panel to Ann Holliday 1753

ST. CLEER

Robert Langford 1614

(Plate 8)

Arms: Paly of six, Argent and Gules on a chief Azure, a lion passant guardant Or.

Position: At the east end of the south aisle behind the organ.

Size: 6 feet 6 inches by 3 feet.

Condition: Very badly worn and part of the carving obliterated. No doubt formerly set in the floor, now cemented on a stone " chest " and covered by a thick cloth.

Style: Inside a badly worn border inscription is a narrow panel containing a Latin inscription which divides the stone into two sections. On the left-hand side is incised the figure of Robert Langford kneeling on a cushion before a prayer stool; his wife kneels behind him. Between them is a shield bearing the arms of Langford and in the left corner a skull and in the right corner an hour-glass. Above is a Latin inscription. The man wears a ruff and long tunic with hanging sleeves. The woman has on a small-brimmed hat and a simple full-skirted gown.

The other half of the slate shows the kneeling figures of Emmanuel, son and heir of Robert, and his wife Alice. Between them is a worn shield and a Latin phrase. Below are the kneeling figures of their nine children, four sons and five daughters. The initials of each child still remain.

Inscription: Robertus Langeford armiger decessit 23 of February Ao Dom 1614 Emanuel Lang . . . Robt decessed . . . Petronilla uxor Roberti Langeford dece . . . suffer little children & forbid them not to com unto me for of such is ye Kingdom of heaven. Memento mori: aetatis sua 80: virtute non vi aetat suaeutmora sicvita. subspe resurrec tionis ubi momen. ibi numen

The remaining letters are partly defaced.

Fixed on the wall beside this tomb is a slate tablet measuring 3 feet by 2 feet whereon is inscribed the " Langford Creed " thus:

It is my will that those almes be given unto poore people that can make testimony of there faith, not for merit but for Christe sake, and learne this question following. quest. What ys your faith in Christ? answ. I believe when Adam through temtation of the divell fell from God to sinne & wickednes, our Saviour Jesus Christ came down fro' heaven, & by his just life did fulfill the lawe in man's behalf, & on good friday died upon the crosse to pay the debt & ransome for man's syn, to pacifie God's wrath, & to reconcile man againe unto him; all this doe I steadfastly beleve that Christ hath done for me; & I am certenly assured

St. Cleer
Robert Langford 1614

Plate 8

upon my true repentance yt the whole worke of my redemption
is as frely wrought in me by his death as though I had done it
myselfe; this my faith, wherein I hope to be saved.

faith, hope & love, the three-folde coarde of life,
devided by the fatall sisters' knife.
To Saintes & men on earth, god in heaven,
thus tri-partite hath ancient Langeford given.
whose alms-deeds, vigils, embers, praiers, & teares,
nu'berd his howres, his daies, months, weekes & yeares.
And with his fortunes—numbers did accorde;
much spent, much lent, forgiven & restor'd.
which he received in heaven with the Just:
Lo there his spirit lives,—heere lyes his dust.[1]

Robert Langford of Tremabe was the second son of Henry Langford
of Langford, Devon.   He married Petronell, daughter of Stephen
Andrew alias Hooper, and by her had 3 sons and 4 daughters. Emmanuel
who was the third and only surviving son, married Alice, daughter of
George Cary of Clovelly Devon and by her had five sons, four of whom
are recorded on the slate: Francis, Edward, Robert and Emmanuel.
Of their seven daughters five are represented: Elizabeth, Priscilla,
Grace, Mary and Julyan.   John, Dorothy and Katherine are not re-
membered.[2]

Tremabe lies about a mile south of the church and a few yards back
from the main road.   A modern house now occupies the site.

---

[1] The late Mr. Edwin Chirgwin writing in " Old Cornwall " gives an account of some most
interesting researches he made into the setting up of the Langford charity, and its ultimate end:
   In 1613 an Indenture was made between Robert Langford of Tremabe and his son Emmanuel
of the one party, and Sir William Wrey of Trebygh, Knight and William Coryton of Newton Esq.
of the other part, " for the Charitable love which they beare unto the poore inhabitants within
the Parish of St. Cleere."
   But Samuel must have been imbued with the same generous feelings as his ancestor, for he
had another Indenture drawn up in which the same amount of 34/8 yearly was to become available
from " those lands and tenements called Gymble also Gymmoll in the aforesaid Parish of St.
Cleere, containing about 34 acres of land forever."
   Sir William Wrey and William Coryton were appointed as Trustees of the Charity which was
to provide 34/8 the annual rent of Torr Park, to be spent in eightpennyworth of bread for each
of 52 poor persons who could make confession of the Langford Creed. Robert Langford died the
next year 1614 and was buried in St. Cleer church and the " creed " was then cut on the slate
tablet and placed on the wall above, as it is now. The Charity was administered for the next
72 years until, in 1685, Samuel Langford, great-grandson of Robert, sold Torr Park.
   Samuel Langford apparently died without a male heir, for the Charity lapsed in 1707 and more
than twenty years passed before the Church wardens and Overseers of the Parish combined in
endeavouring to revive the Charity, by threat of prosecution of the new owner of Gymble to
pay the accumulation of the yearly sum of 34/8d. As the owner of the land resolutely refused
to be held thus responsible, the Parish authorities decided that the matter was not worth the cost
of a lawsuit and so ended the Langford Charity which had lasted only 93 years
[2] *Visitations C.*, p. 278,

Plate 9   ST. COLUMB MINOR
Elizabeth Pollamounter 1640

ST. COLUMB MINOR

Elizabeth Pollamounter 1640

(Plate 9)

Arms: Azure, a sea-lion Argent.

Position: On the north wall of the nave.

Size: 2 feet 6 inches by 1 foot 6 inches.

Condition: Fair. A light grey rather soft slate shows signs of weathering.

Style: Set within a border inscription is the full-length figure of a young woman wearing a low-necked gown and large brimmed bonnet, prettily tied with ribbons and a flower. The lettering is good though badly spaced.

Inscription: Here lyeth Elizabeth ye daughter of Richard Pollamounter Esq. buried February the 14 1640

The family of Pollamounter was formerly seated in Newlyn East before removing to Trevithick in St. Columb Minor.

At the present farm some of the old house remains, in the kitchen quarters and the stone pillars set at the entrance to the old carriage way. Trevithick remained in the possession of the Pollamounters until towards the middle of the 18th century.

Roger Ellery 1640

(Plate 10)

Position: On the north wall of the nave.

Size: 2 feet 7 inches by 2 feet 2 inches.

Condition: Good.

Style: Very crudely carved, in low relief, is the full-length figure of a man wearing the dress of James I reign and with the letters R.E. boldly displayed across his breeches. The figure stands beneath an arch upon which is carved:—

Inscription: " MORS MEA EST VITA MIHI "

The family of Ellery has been resident in the parish for several centuries, and as in each generation there appeared a Roger Ellery, there seems little doubt but that it was a man of that name who is carved on the slate.

In his will dated 1640[1] Roger Ellery described himself as . . . " the unprofitable servant of God . . ." and after a somewhat lengthy discourse upon his faith in the goodness and mercy of his Creator, goes on

[1] C.R.O., wills.

Plate 10   St. Columb Minor
Roger Ellery 1640

to bequeath the sum of three shillings and fourpence " . . . toward the repayring of the church of Collumbe minor and to the poore peopell of the same parish ten shillings . . ."

A further bequest is ". . . unto some goode and godly Divine whom my executrixs shall think goode with the consent of the minister for the preaching of a sermon in the church of St. Columb the Lower on the Sunday called St. Columb Feast Day in the afternoon and I doe give him for his paynes therein 6/8 and the same to be continued for the space of seven years next after my death . . ."

Roger Ellery farmed at Porthvean and left a wife, Agnes, two daughters and four sons of whom Roger was appointed " Register "[2] during the Commonwealth in 1655, and after the Restoration became Parish Clerk. This appointment continued in the family for several generations.

CREED

Thomas and Henry Denys 1570 1602

Arms: Ermine, 3 battle axes Gules.

Position: At the east end of the south aisle.

Size: 6 feet 6 inches by 2 feet 3 inches.

Condition: Fairly good except for a break across the top end.

Style: A slate panel now cemented to a concrete base. It is divided into three sections: at the top is the inscription; then a shield and crest, elaborately carved in bold relief showing the arms of Denys impaling Tremayne, and below, some lines of poor verse.

Inscription: Here lye the bodyes of Thomas Denys Gentlemen who died ye 26th of August 1589: and of Maron his wife, ye daughter of Thomas Tremayne of Colocombe esquire She dyed ye 11th daye of April 1570: and of Henry Denys their son bachelor of ye civil law who dyed ye 13th day of September 1602:

Here is the ende of all
Heere lo the patern prest before your eyes
Is layde to meete whereto at length you shall
The greatest monarche dead even this he lyeth
ende then your sinninge ere ye end of all
of riche or poore of men in vale of blis
All one shalbe ye end take (heed) by this

Thomas Dennis (Denys) was the second son of Henry Dennis of Petrockestowe in Devon. He married Margaret, a daughter of Thomas Tremayne of Collacombe, and by her had six sons and two daughters. The eldest son, Henry, died in 1602, as recorded on the slate, and the descent continued through the third son Thomas, who became Rector of Menheniot.[1]

---

[2] See W. E. Tate, *The Parish Chest*, p. 46.
[1] *Visitations C.*, p. 138.

CROWAN

Richard Tregeare 1668

Arms: Argent, a fess Sable between 3 Cornish Choughs proper.
Position: Lying against the wall on the east side of the churchyard.
Size: 5 feet 6 inches by 3 feet.
Condition: One end is broken and the surface lichened from long
exposure to the weather.
Style: Set within a border inscription is a quaintly worded verse·
Separated from the rhyme by a column, is a shield displaying the arms
of Tregeare and surrounded by a bold leaf and scroll design.   The
bottom left-hand corner is filled with a fleur-de-lis.
Inscription: Here lyeth the Body of Richard Tregeare of this
Parish, Gentl. who departed this life in the fear of God the
24th day of December Anno 1668.

> Why here? Why not? 'tis Holy Ground;
> And here none will my Dust Confound.
> My Saviour lay where no one did,
> Why not a Member as his Head?
> No Quire to Sing, no Bell to Ring!
> Why Sirs! thus Buried was my King!
> My King in Joseph's Garden lay;
> Why may not I in the Church lay?
> And that I might be Neerer yet,
> I would as He was, neer Sun set.
> I Grudge the fashion of this day,
> To fat the Church and Starve the lay.
> Though Nothing now of me be seen,
> I Hope my Name and bed is Green.

Richard Tregeare fil posuit in Honorem patr; & Memor.
Tregeare lies about one mile south of the church, and it is now a
modern farmhouse.   The family of Tregeare became extinct in 1732.

CUBERT

Arthur and Humphrey Lawrence 1669 1699

Arms: Argent, a cross raguly Gules, on a chief of the second a lion
passant Or.
Position: Fixed to the south wall of the chancel inside the altar rail.
Size: 5 feet 7 inches by 2 feet 9 inches.
Condition: Perfect.   Cleaned and replaced in 1833 by Northmore
Lawrence Esq.
Style: In a protective frame of stone, and carved in low relief.   The
Latin inscription is set between two leaf-patterned pilasters which

support a panel of elaborately carved detail: the centre-piece is a chalice
with a scalloped cover, a winged angel's head and a rose carved on the
bowl. A bold pattern of flowers and foliage surround the cup, and a skull
and crossed bones are at its base. A smaller panel of leaf pattern is set
at the bottom of the slate.

Inscription:

M.P.Q.S.
Hic Juxta Positae
Jacent Exuvioe
Arthuri Lawrence Plebei,
sed animo generosi:
Nec non Humfridi filii Quarto-geniti
Patri in omnibus simillimi
In manum Dei depositae:
Qui non natalibus aut stemmate Genilitio
fuere Spectabiles,
Sed probitate vitae et moribus inculpatis
Inter Primos.
Bonis omnibus flebiles occidere
Ut vixere Amabiles.
Resurgent: Quando? Tantem.
Hoc officii et Pietatis Ergo posuit
Tho: Lawrence Cler. filius unice superstes
Arthurus abiit Aprilis 19, 1669
Humfridu' Junii 9, 1699.[1]

Arthur Lawrence died in 1669, and his son Humphrey in 1699.
Humphrey's brother, Thomas, who became vicar of St. Winnow,
erected the slate and also brought up and educated the three orphan
children of Humphrey. One of these children, Arthur, became an
attorney and settled at Launceston,[2] and it was his descendant, Northmore Lawrence, who in 1833 had the slate cleaned and restored.

In his will dated 1668[3] Arthur Lawrence, described as yeomen of the
parish of Cubert, bequeathed "... unto my wife Joan Lawrence one
bedd ffully furnished which she shall make choyse of ... unto my
Eldest Sonn Thomas Lawrence my silver salt being gilded and my best
Dozen of silver spoons and my Gould ring and threescore pounds in
money whereof are ten pounds thereof to be paid by quarterly payments
the ffirst yeare after my Decease ... I give unto my sonn Arthur
Lawrence one Dozen of silver spoons and a silver Bowlle and my
ffrench Gunn. I give unto my sonn Humphrey Lawrence one Dozen
of silver spoons and a silver Cupp ... I give unto my Apprentice
servant John Duncaster twenty shillings."

Arthur and Humphrey further inherited their father's lands, in the
parish of Padstow, and the rest of his goods and chattels and were
ordained to be joint executors of the will.

[1] *Lake,* Vol. I, p. 275.
[2] *Visitations C.,* p. 592.
[3] C.R.O.

Plate 11   DULOE
Ann Smith 1592

DULOE
Ann Smith 1592
(Plate 11)

Arms: Azure, a saltire Argent between four martlets Or.

Position: Attached to the north wall of the Colshill Chapel.

Size: 5 feet 4 inches by 2 feet 6 inches. A coffin-shaped slab.

Condition: Very good. Slight damage to face of effigy.

Style: Inside a narrow border with a Latin inscription is carved in relief the full-length figure of a woman. She wears a high-crowned hat and ruff, with a richly patterned gown, and carries in one hand a pair of gloves and in the other a prayer book. Behind her head are two shields, displaying Tremayne impaling Coffin, and Smith impaling Coffin. In the space between her large feet is carved " Memento Mori " and a skull.

> *Inscription:* Anna filia Richardi Coffyn ar. vidua Rogeri Tremayne ar. caepit in virum Johannem Smyth, gen. ejusque uxor, obiit primo die martii, Anno Domini millessimo Quingentessimo Nonagessimo Secundo.

Ann was the eldest daughter, and one of the nine children of Richard and Wilmot Coffin of Portledge in Devon. She first married Roger Tremayne, son of Thomas Tremayne of Collacombe, at Lamerton on 1st February 1550—1. By him she had one son John, who died an infant, and four daughters, the eldest of whom, Phillippa, married Hannibal Vivian of Trelowarren.[1]

After the death of Roger Tremayne in March 1571—2, Ann married John Smith of Lanwarnick in Duloe, the second son of Robert Smith of Tregonack in St. Germans. By this marriage she became aunt to her daughter Wilmot, who had married Thomas Smith a grandson of Robert.[2]

Lanwarnick lies two miles west of the church.

Mary Arundell 1629
(Plate 12)

Arms: Sable, six swallows, 3, 2 and 1 Argent.

Position: On the north wall of the Colshill Chapel.

Size: 5 feet 5 inches by 2 feet 6 inches.

Condition: Good. Slight damage to face of larger figure.

Style: A most interesting monument, as it has carved on it in low relief, two full-length female figures, yet commemorating only one person. Both figures are coarsely drawn and set side by side, with a shield of arms between them showing Arundell impaling Cary. The

[1] *Visitations C.,* p. 617.
[2] *Visitations C.,* p. 427.

Plate 12   DULOE

Mary Arundell 1629

smaller figure, wearing a long loose gown and a bonnet, is apparently
that of a little child; and when considered with the verse set out below,
may imply that Mary made a miraculous recovery from a serious
illness when an infant, but died suddenly while still very young. The
larger figure is similarly dressed but wears the traditional French hood.
Surrounding the figures and epitaph is a border inscription and an outer
band of decoration.

    Inscription: Here lyeth the body of Marye Arundell the daughter
    of Thomas Arundell Esquire who was buried the 8th day of
    June Anno 1629

Maria Arundell
Man a dry Laurell
Man to the marigold compared may bee
Man may be lik'nd to the laurell tree
Both feed the eye,—both please the optick sense
Both soon decay,—both suddenly fleet hence,
What then infere you from her name but this
Man fades away: man a dry laurell is.
Jairus yong daughter found as fair a path
To her long home as old Methusalah
Not beautye, youth: not sex or higth of fate
But young, or old that with his golden head
Salutes the sunne may with the sunne fall dead.
I once did live, but ere I lived in light
I tooke my leave and bid the world good night.

Mary Arundell was the young daughter of Thomas Arundell Esquire
of Tremadart, and niece of John Arundell Esquire of Trerice, the Gover-
nor and defender of Pendennis Castle at its surrender in the Civil War.[3]

Tremadart was the most important of the several manors in the
parish: the Lords of Tremadart were, until the beginning of the 18th
century, patrons of the living, when it passed to Balliol College Oxford.
The old house at Tremadart has gone and a farm now occupies the site,
about three-quarters of a mile north-west of the church.

(Plate 13)

Position: On the wall under the east window of the Colshill Chapel.

Size: 6 feet by 3 feet.

Condition: Excellent.

Style: Set within an elaborately carved border are two female figures,
kneeling on cushions and facing each other across a large prayer desk.
The woman on the right wears the standing ruff and wide-brimmed hat
of an early Jacobean lady, and kneeling behind her are two daughters
wearing bonnets. The second child has a skull carved above her head
and was therefore already deceased.

³ *Visitations C.*, p. 12.

D

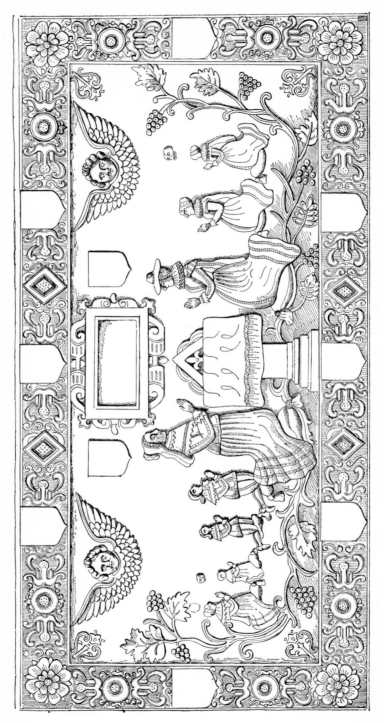

DULOE

Plate 13

The woman on the opposite side wears a loose draping over her hair and the falling collar of Charles I period. Two of her sons wear their hair long and have collars like their mother; the other two male infants were deceased; one showing a skull above its head, the other with the trace of one removed. A large trailing vine along the base and sides of the figures, and above them a tablet, two shields and cherubs heads complete the design.

The identity of this family is unknown as all the shields and the tablet are blank, and although this slate would appear to be part of a tomb-chest, there is no evidence of such a tomb having been in the church.

An approximate date for this monument is 1640. The figures may represent two wives and their children, or a mother and daughter, as there is a difference of about twenty years shown in the styles of dress.

EGLOSKERRY

William Saltren 1742

Arms: Azure, a lion rampant within an orle of mullets, Argent.

Position: Attached to the north wall of the nave.

Size: 4 feet 4 inches by 2 feet 7 inches.

Condition: Excellent.

Style: Carved in low relief at the top of the tablet are the arms of Saltren. The lettering is very good and the name of the carver is shown; John Burt, Callington.

Inscription: Here underneath lyeth the body of William Saltren Esq. son of John Saltren Esq. and Elizabeth his wife, of Tre-ludick in this parish, who departed this life the 22nd day of April 1742 aetatis suae 27.

This slate was recorded in 1867 as being " attached to the east end of the church on the outside "[1] and there is no doubt that it was originally there, for in his will[2] made on 9th June 1740, when he was already a sick man, William Saltren directed that his body ". . . be decently interred in Egloskerry Churchyard outside the window against my seat at the East End of the Church, a Tomb to be fixed on the Grave at the Discretion of my Executrix . . . my dear sister Anna Saltren."

A bench at the East end of the aisle is still known as the Treludick seat.

William, who died unmarried, was the eldest of six children and in his will he remembers his widowed mother with the gift of ". . . one Diamond Ring of the value of Three Guineas." His brothers, Christopher, with " My Best Pair of Silver Buckles and Knee Buckles," and

[1] Lake, Vol. I, p. 325.
[2] C.R.O., Wills.

Thomas with " . . . one Guinea, and my old pair of Silver Buckles and Knee Buckles and a Silver Salver." His wearing apparel was to be divided equally between the two. His brother John inherited the estate, and Anna his goods and chattels.

Treludick remains as a charming Elizabethan house, two miles west of the church, low-built on the E plan with central block and projecting wings. Two of the ground-floor rooms are panelled and have moulded plaster ceilings. Some Jacobean carved panels can be seen above the stairs. An outbuilding has a stone arched doorway on which is carved J. B. 1641. Treludick first belonged to the Baron family of Tregeare, passing to the Saltrens by the marriage of William's grandfather, William Saltren of St. Ive, to Joan Baron in 1682.

John Carne 1624

Position: In the south porch.

Size: 5 feet 8 inches by 3 feet.

Condition: Rather worn; broken at edges.

Style: A panel bearing an epitaph and crudely drawn angel's head, surrounded by an inscription and decorated border. The unusual design of the border is carved in low relief and shows the figures of a mermaid (holding a mirror and comb), a horse, a unicorn, and a rose.

Inscription: Here lyeth the body of John Carne of Bodharlocke[3] who departed this life the -9 daye of November in the yeere of our Lord God 1624.

As tis uncertaine when Deaths stroke shall fall,
Tis certaine once that it will light on all.
Here Hee doth Sleep, whose vertuous life on Earth
did shine till Death did stopp his vitall breath
(Hee cloth'd the naked, nere did shutt his dore
against the indigent or hungry poore
yet Deedes of pitty reach not to his love
He inuir'd none, his heart was fixt above.)
but though his Corps wth worms be turn'd to mould
His soule wth Angels doth Gods face behould
When not A Barne on Earth
Earth's corn shall hide
This Barne in heaven shalbe reedefiede
(a glorious Temple ever to remaine)
and there enioy ye the never fading graine.

---

[3] D. & C. N. & Q., Vol. XXVII, pt. XII, p. 331.

ST. ENODER

Dorothy Tanner 1634

(Plate 14)

Arms: Argent, on a chief Sable, three mens heads Or.

Position: Fixed to the north wall of the north chancel aisle.

Size: 5 feet 7 inches by 3 feet.

Condition: Well preserved except for damaged portion of bottom left-hand corner.

Style: The inscription is set across the top of this black slate, which is divided by ornamented pilasters into two parts. On the right side, under a semi-circular pediment, are crudely carved in low relief, the kneeling figures of a woman and her two children. A chrisom infant lies in the foreground.[1]

On the left, under a second pediment, is a quaint verse wherein it will be noticed that the letter " S " is cut in reverse. Three shields complete the design, displaying: the arms of Tanner; Tanner impaling Arundell; and a shield lozengy.

Inscription: Heere lyeth ye Body of Dorothye ye wiefe of Anthony Tanner, gent., daughter of Zachary Arundell, of this parishe, gent., who departed this life in the feare of God, the 2 day of February 1634.

> God nere repeents of what he hath given to men;
> And yet he geives, and yet he takes agen
> What he had geiven; as here in her we trye,
> Who was the gift of God,—a Dorothye.
> God gave her to her parents, next he gave her
> Unto her husband,—and when he will have her
> To be his owne, again resign they doe
> What for a time they had a right unto:
> And yet to showe shee was not geiven in vaine,
> Before he takes her to himselfe againe,
> By her he geives them two for one, that shee
> Might quitte her being on earth with usurye,
> Two modells of her selfe she leaves b'hinde her
> . . . them her friends (though dead) might find her
> . . . God and such his mercye to us
> . . . ts when he seems to undoe us.

Dorothy was the daughter and heiress of Zachary Arundell, a younger branch of the great Lanherne family, and a third son, as shown by the mullet displayed on the Arundell coat. Married at about eighteen to Anthony, third son of Anthony Tanner of Court in St. Stephen-in-

---

[1] Introduction, p. 5.

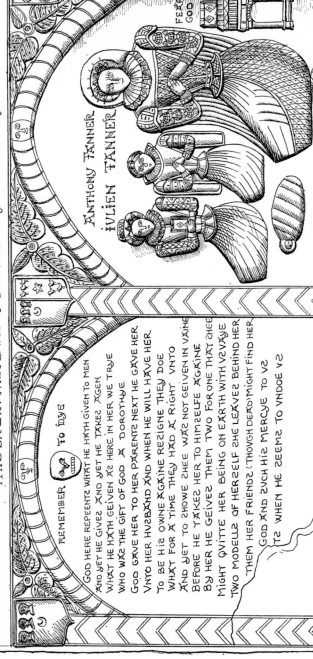

Plate 14

ST. ENODER
Dorothy Tanner 1634

Brannel: Dorothy bore her husband two children, a daughter Julian and a son Anthony, and died with the birth of a third child four years after her marriage.

Julian Tanner married Matthew Vivian of Trethan in Advent and had one son and three daughters.

Anthony Tanner married Grace, a daughter of Thomas Carthew of Canaligy in St. Issey, and had one son.[2]

The family of Tanner was seated at Carvynack in St. Enoder. The house, built in 1669 by Anthony the son of Dorothy, lies about a mile west from the church. It still retains some of the old building, including a stone carved with the initials of Anthony and his wife Grace.

ST. ENODOC
John and Alice Mably 1687
(Plate 15)

Position: On the north-east side of the churchyard.

Size: 6 feet by 3 feet.

Condition: Very poor. Badly broken and roughly joined by iron staples. From continued exposure to the weather the stone has become heavily lichened and stained.

Style: A red brick base with a slate top, the only one of its kind remaining outside a church. Inside a border inscription are the two incised figures of John Mably and his young daughter Alice. Crudely cut, the man's figure is shown dressed in a simple tunic with cravat and knee breeches and wearing his hair long. The girl has a kerchief on her head, and her dress has a laced bodice and hooped skirt. The lettering, although very simple, is distinguished by the carver's quaint fancy for decoration in the drawing of tiny faces within the capital letters.

Inscription: John Mably was Buried The 24th Day of July 1687
Alice Mably was Buried The 30th Day of July 1687
      remember man within thy youthfull days
      to serve the Lord eare death thy body seize
      then Live to dye to came soe high a price
      that thy poore soule may Live in paradise
      the Father and daughter.
      Here is the Love of my wife Shone that where
      wee Ly by this it may be known
      my wife and I did in Love So well a gree
      yet must I part For god
      would have it so to be
      From my wife Ann Mably

John Mably, a prosperous yeoman farmer, was a son of Richard and Edith Mably. He married Ann Guy, and in his will[1] names two children;

[2] *Visitations C.*, p. 447—8.
[1] C.R.O.

Plate 15   ST. ENODOC
John and Alice Mably 1687

Richard (his executor) and Alice who was buried six days after her father.
Although not apparently himself a Quaker, John Mably was both
friendly and sympathetic towards them and appointed John Peters, the
Quaker minister of St. Minver, his " trustee and well beloved friend "
to be an overseer of his will. One of the entries in the inventory of his
goods reads: " Charles Peters and John Peters on bond £20."
A family of Mably still farms at Trebetherick in St. Minver.

ST. ERVAN
William Arthur 1627
(Plate 16)

Position: Set low against the north wall of the north transept.

Size: 5 feet 6 inches by 2 feet 6 inches.

Condition: Fairly good, edges badly broken and part of inscription
missing.

Style: Cut very crudely in low relief within a border inscription are
the kneeling figures of a man and woman with eight children. The man
wears a plain doublet and knee breeches and has a spade beard. Each
of the five boys is dressed the same. The woman and three girls all
wear wide-brimmed hats and have ruffs and simple gowns. Every face
has well marked brows.

Inscription: Here lyeth the Body of William Arthur of this Pish.
    yeoman who was buryed the 14th day of May. Anno Domini
    1627. Hee had issue 5 sonnes And 3 daughters.

Writing in 1882 A. J. Jewers describes this memorial as attached to
a window sill.

William Pomeroy 1622
(Plate 17)

Arms: Or, a lion rampant Gules within a bordure engrailed.

Position: Against the east wall of the south transept.

Size: 5 feet 9 inches by 2 feet 6 inches.

Condition: Good.

Style: Crudely carved in low relief is the full-length figure of a man
wearing a doublet and knee breeches; by his head is a shield displaying
the arms of Pomeroy.

Border Inscription: Here lieth the body of William Pomeroye
    Esquier, who departed this life on the thirde day of Julie An'o
    Domini 1622 Memento Mori.

No record of the estate has so far been traced or to which branch of
the family William Pomeroy belonged, although it would seem most
likely to be that of St. Columb Major; yet the shield of arms displays the
engrailed bordure of the Tregony Pomeroys.

St. Ervan
William Arthur 1627

Plate 16

Plate 17   St. Ervan
                William Pomeroy 1622

Richard Russell 1654

Position: Set low against the south wall of the chancel.

Size: 5 feet 6 inches by 2 feet 6 inches.

Condition: Perfect.

Style: A border inscription set around three sides of a panel; the lower edge is decorated with a pattern of strapwork in low relief. Inside the border is an extravagant epitaph extolling the many virtues of the man who held the living during the Commonwealth. The design is completed with some traditional Elizabethan scrollwork and four stylised flowers.

Inscription: Here lyeth the Body of Richard Russell, Minister of this Parish, who was Buried the eleventh day of December 1654.

Looke on this living Saint, this Matchles summ,
So Comprehensive a Compendium.
A Learned Scholler, Painfull Labourer;
A Faithfull Shepheard, True, Embassadour;
An untir'ed Watchman, & A shining Saint;
A Burning Taper, Beauty without Paint,
Bright Gem has left its casket to be sett,
By God into a Nobler Coronett.
Ripe Grace Now ends in Glory: so is he
Sounding Triumphs with the Hierachy.

Richard Harvey 1666

Position: Against the north wall of the chancel inside the altar rail.

Size: 6 feet by 3 feet.

Condition: Good except for broken edges.

Style: A border inscription set around three sides of an epitaph, and a simple incised pattern of fleur-de-lys and flowers. The lower edge of the panel has been broken off.

Inscription: The body of Richard Harvey, Master of Arts, of Christ's Colledge in Cambridge, and Rector of this Parish, who died the second day of September Anno Domini 1666.

Here doth the body lie that earthly masse
Returned is to dust, as first it was;
But his Diviner part, his Purer Spiritt
Is flown aloft, and heaven doth in heritt,
What of great Basill once was sayd, the same
May be of him, to his Immortall fame.
He Thundred in his doctrine, and with all,
Hee lightened in his life Angelicall.
Fought a good fight, he hath ranne well his race
And kept the faith; now by the Allmightie's grace

Hee weares the Crowne, shining a starre most bright
Amonge these glorious saints above in light.

The window in the south wall of the chancel may have been put in
by Richard Harvey, as his initials and the date 1665 are carved in
granite on the outside wall.

The Parsonage House is described in a Terrier of 1727[1] as being
built and covered with slate stones, with the exception of two ground
floor rooms with three little rooms over, which were of stone and covered
with thatch. In all there were fifteen rooms, two little cellars, a malt
room and brewhouse.

The present Rectory was built about a century ago.

(*Plate 18*)

Stapled to the south wall, at the west end of the nave, is a fragment
of slate measuring roughly twenty inches square. Carved on it in low
relief, are the kneeling figures of a boy and girl and one corner of a
border inscription. Part of a name can be traced which is interpreted as
William Hawkey.

This piece of slate is all that remains of a panel carved with a family
group.

ST. EVAL

Simon and Elinor Leach 1672 1687

Arms: Ermine, on a chief indented Gules three ducal coronets Or.

Position: Fixed to the west wall of the transept.

Size: 5 feet 10 inches by 2 feet 11 inches.

Condition: Excellent.

Style: Skilfully carved in low relief, the inscription is set within an
oval, supported by two ornamented pilasters. The two top spaces are
filled on each side by a clenched hand holding a spray of leaves. In the
centre is a winged angel's head carved in great detail. Above is set a
shield of arms, Leach impaling Trevithick, and the crest, a hand
grasping a serpent. The remaining space is filled with sun-like faces,
urns and flowers. This slate is one of the most elaborate and best carved
of the decorative kind, and could be by the same hand as that which
worked the Toker slate at Blisland.

Inscription: In memory of Simon Leach, gent., who was buried
the 19th day of March Anno Dom 1672 also Elinor his wife,
who was buried the 12th day of November Anno Dom 1687;
Mary therie fifth daughter who was buried the 11th May,
Anno Dom 1707; and Thomasin, theire eldest daughter, who
was buried the 7th of September, Anno Dom. 1709.

---

[1] C.R.O. Although 60 years later, this might still have been a fair description of the Vicarage
of Richard Harvey.

Plate 18   ST. ERVAN
Remnant of panel to Hawkey family

Simon Leach married Elinor Trevithick of Trevemider in St. Eval in 1631. His house and manor of Trethewell lie a mile north from the church. Trethewell in the middle ages was a place of considerable magnificence. A few pieces of 14th and 15th century carved stonework alone remain to mark its former grandeur. Some old brick buildings (late 18th century) made of bricks manufactured on the estate were probably erected when the Leach family resided here.[1]

The present house is comparatively modern, but the courtyard walls of brick remain and the gate posts surmounted by a pair of weatherworn unicorns.[2]

GRADE

Hugh Mason 1671

Arms: Azure, a fess embattled between 3 griffins heads erased Or.

Position: Attached to the north wall of the chancel, on the outside.

Size: 6 feet 9 inches by 3 feet 5 inches.

Condition: Fairly good.

Style: Carved in low relief, the family crest and arms are in a cartouche above a curious verse and set within a border inscription.

Inscription: Here lyeth the body of Hugh Mason gentleman, who departed this life in the fear of God, the third day of December 1671 and at the age of 65.

> Why here? why not? 'tis all one ground,
> And here none will my dust confound.
> My Saviour lay where no one did;
> Why not a member as his head?
> No quire to sing, no bells to ring?
> Why, Sirs, thus buried was my King!
> I grudge the fashion of this day,
> To fat the church and starve the lay:
> Though nothing now of me be seene
> I hope my name and bed is greene.[3]

This slate was originally the top portion of a tomb-chest which stood nearby. It seems likely that this was the first burial on the north side of the churchyard, at that time regarded with much disfavour and superstition.

Hugh Mason of Gwavas was the third son of Richard Mason. He is described as a merchant when, in 1654, he purchased of Michael

[1] Henderson, Vol. III, p. 90.
[2] Arms of Trevithick.
[3] A shorter version of the inscription to Richard Tregeare at Crowan (Q.V.).

Tresahar for £105 all his lands in Leazarde.[4] He had two sons, William and John, and a daughter Jane. In his will[5] Hugh bequeaths to his beloved wife Dorcas, an annuity of £12 yearly unless she " shall take and accept of her Dyet and entertaynement with my Executor— " (her son William) when she was to receive only £4. An interesting entry in the inventory of goods reads: " Salt in the cellar at Helfoard £23."

Gwavas lies half a mile south of the church and a few yards from the road. Many alterations and modern additions have changed the character of the old house. Part of the courtyard wall remains, and in the kitchen the open fireplace with cloam ovens is intact.

HELLAND

Humfrey Calwodely

(Plate 19)

Arms: Azure, a pair of wings in lure Argent, over a fess Gules.

Position: Set in the floor of the south aisle near the organ.

Size: 5 feet 8 inches by 2 feet 9 inches.

Condition: Very worn, carving scarcely legible.

Style: Inside a border inscription is the incised, full-length, figure of a man wearing a loose gown with hanging sleeves. Two shields display the arms of Calwodely; and Calwodely impaling Carminow.

Inscription: Yow shall praye for the sowle of Humfrey Calwodely son and ayre of Thomas Calwodely & Eliz. daughter & ayre to Otes Colyn.

Humphrey, son and heir of Thomas Calwodely of Calwodely in Devon supported the rebellion by Perkin Warbeck in 1497, for which he was attainted, convicted of treason and his lands (which included the Manor of Helland with the advowson of the Church) forfeited. He married Johanna, daughter of John Carminow of Fentongollen and widow of John Pentyre Jnr.

In 1506, the Act of Attainder, so far as it affected Humphrey Calwodely, was reversed in favour of Joan, his eldest surviving daughter, and in 1508 there was a further reversal with restoration in blood and possessions to her. In this last record Humphrey is described as deceased, so he evidently died between these two dates.[1]

⁴ Henderson, Vol. II.
⁵ C.R.O.
¹ Maclean, Vol. II, p. 8.

Plate 19 HELLAND

Humfrey Calwodely *circa* 1500

St. Ive

Figured panels from the tomb of Blanche and John Wrey 1597 (at Tawstock, Devon)

Plate 20

ST. IVE

Blanche and John Wrey 1595 1597

(Plate 20)

Arms: Sable, a fess between 3 pole-axes Argent helved Gules.

Position: In the north transept of Tawstock Church, Devon.

Size: Approx, 14 feet by 6 feet

Condition: Very good.

Style: This slate tomb-chest, with elaborate backplate, is carved in bold relief and originally stood in the chancel of St. Ive Church before removal to Tawstock in 1924.

The backplate is arranged in three panels. The smallest, at the top, displays a shield of ten quarterings with a crest, and eight smaller shields at its base.

The second panel is larger, and has three shields of arms carved between a lavish decoration of fruit and cherubs, still bearing traces of colour, mostly yellow.

The third panel shows the figure of John Wrey, bearded, wearing a ruff and suit of armour. He kneels on a tiny cushion before a prayer stool with a Bible on it, and beside him is a shield with the arms of Wrey. The stool is carved with a quaint, almost jaunty figure (of himself?) being stabbed by Death with his dart. Behind the man is the kneeling figure of his mother wearing traditional head-dress, ruff and brocaded gown. Beside her is a shield displaying the Arwenack quartering of the Killigrew arms. The two figures are set within a frame decorated with scrolls and strapwork.

Considerable traces of colour remain in the flesh tints, the blue gown with red trimmings and gold jewellery; some red on the armour and the yellow sword tassels. The drawing of the figures is very like that of William and Jane Vyell at St. Breock and most probably the work of the same carver.

On the top panel of the chest is a border inscription. The front panel is divided by a pilaster on which is carved a figure with folded arms. On the left side is a shield of Wrey impaling Arwenack, and on the right a similar shield of Wrey impaling Smyth. Each shield is set below a curved pediment ornamented and coloured yellow. The end panel displays the arms of Wrey.

Attached to the monument are two panels, one on the left bearing the epitaph, and the other, on the right, the kneeling figure of a man in armour.

A drawing of this monument in C. S. Gilbert's Parochial History of Cornwall Vol. II shows these two slabs set one above the other and surmounted by a third panel with an inscription.

These side panels formed part of the tomb of John Wrey, the husband of Blanche, who died at Bridestowe in 1576.[1] The carved figure has at some time been coated with a coloured distemper.

Inscription: Heere lyeth the body of Blaunch Wrey, who was buried ye 16 of December 1595, and ye body of John Wrey, Esquier, who was buried ye 9th of June Ano.Domini 1597.

Loe here he lieth, though dead yet living still;
His famious name resounding ekoes aye,
Whereby report of hym the ayre doth fyll.,
the lastlinge fame & name of rightfull Wreye.
Good to ye poore,—bribes never would he take,
Voyde of oppression all kind of waye.
He faithful fryends of enemyes did make.
of quarrels greate ceast lawe eche daye by daye.
Death doe thy worst, this Wreye yet lives & shall,
thy darte his deeds cannot extyrpe or quayle.
Thousands are the which thou haste causde to fall
& yet on hym no waye thou canste prevayle.
what resteth then, but cease to mourne & moane
for hym, whose vertues shyne like to the sonne?
Though here he lieth, his soul to heaven is gone
where angells see hym though his threade be spunne.
And the body of John Wrey.

John Wrey of Trebigh was the son of Walter Wrey of North Russell in Devonshire. He married Blanche, daughter and co-heiress of Henry Killigrew of Wolston, and by her had six sons and two daughters. In his will, dated September 27th 1575[2], John bequeathed to each of his two daughters, Jane Coryton and Phillipa Upton, " three old angells "[3] and to five of his sons, William, Edmund, Robert, George and Arthur, a share in his lands in Devon and at Trebigh. His wife Blanche and his eldest son John, appointed co-executors, inherited the residue of all his lands and property.

John Wrey Esq., eldest son of John and Blanche Wrey, married Elinor, daughter and heir of Bernard Smith of Totnes. He died without issue in 1597 and his estates passed to his brother William.[4]

Trebigh lies in a fertile and pleasantly wooded valley within half a mile west of the church. The manor of Trebigh belonged in pre-reformation days to the Knights Hospitallers of St. John and enjoyed many privileges, including freedom from tithe. John Wrey acquired the estate through his marriage with Blanch Killigrew.

The present farmhouse retains some evidence of the old Wrey mansion, mainly in the east wing now used for storing grain. An old right-of-way established by the Knights still exists, leading from the manor to the church.

[1] D. & C. N. & Q., Vol. XXV, pt. VI, p. 149.
[2] P.C.C. wills.
[3] Gold coins approximate value 6/8 each.
[4] *Visitations C.*, p. 564.

ST. KEW
Honor Webber 1601
(Plate 21)

Arms: Gules, on a chevron engrailed Or between 3 hurts, as many annulets Azure.

Position: Set low against the wall of the north aisle.[1]

Size: 5 feet 10 inches by 1 foot 10 inches.

Condition: Very good. In its present position, one end of the slate and part of the inscription is obscured by water pipes.

Style: Set within a border inscription is the full-length figure of a woman, carved in relief, wearing a hooped but unusually short dress to show the embroidered stockings above her shoes. Below the mother are carved her two sons, kneeling on cushions, and beneath them her daughter also kneeling; the arm of this figure has flaked off.

Inscription: Heere lyeth ye Body of honor wife of John Webber of Ambel daughter to John calwoodley Esquire of Padsto. who died ye VIth of october 1601 and had issue honor Richard Matthu.

Honor was the first wife of John Webber and died after the birth of her youngest son Matthew, who was baptised on 25th September 1601. Richard matriculated at Exeter College Oxford in 1621 and Matthew in 1623, each at the age of 19.[2]

In his will dated 1636,[3] John Webber gave five pounds to each son and desired his executrix (his second wife Susan) to give " each of them Dyett for one whole yeare next after my Death if she please and they will accept thereof." His daughter Honor, and her three half-sisters each inherited a legacy of three hundred pounds, she being still unmarried at the time of her father's death and then aged about 37.

KILKHAMPTON
Sarah Cottell 1727
(Plate 22)

Arms: Or, a bend Gules.

Position: Set low against the wall of the north aisle.

Size: 5 feet 2 inches by 3 feet.

Condition: Excellent.

Style: In the classical fashion of the 18th century marble monuments. At the top are carved in low relief the arms and crest of Cottell, supported by elaborate leaf scrolls and the winged heads of two cherubs. The well-lettered inscription is framed by draped curtains, and at the foot

---

[1] Maclean, Vol. II, p. 107. Formerly a sill in a window.
[2] *Visitations C.*, p. 550.
[3] C.R.O. wills.

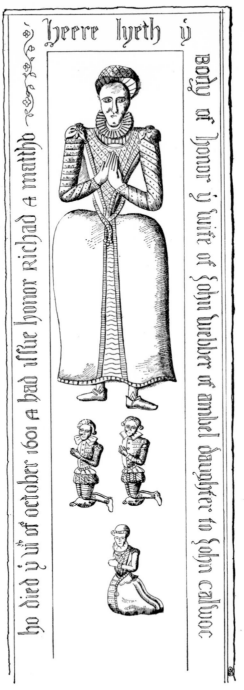

Plate 21   ST. KEW
Honor Webber 1601

HERE

Lyeth the Body of Sarah y^e Wife of Alex^r Cottell of Aldercombe in this Parish Gent who departed this life y^e 7th of August 1727 in y^e 30th year of her age

Plate 22 KILKHAMPTON
Sarah Cottell 1727

a female figure, wrapped in a loose robe, reclines with her head resting awkwardly on one hand. On her left hand she wears a wedding ring. Slight traces of colour remain on the shield and the curtain fringes. This well carved slate is the work of Michael Chuke, a local carver and pupil of Grinling Gibbons.[1]

Inscription: Here lyeth the Body of Sarah ye Wife of Alexr. Cottell of Aldercombe in this Parish Gent. who departed this life ye 7th of August 1727 in ye 30th year of her age.

Aldercombe lies about a mile east of the church; a delightful little Tudor house, set around a courtyard garden and with a fine arched gateway. Aldercombe was for many years held on lease for lives by the family of Cottell. Mr. Alexander Cottell, of this place, about the year 1720, having served his clerkship in Penzance as an attorney, married Sarah, daughter of Mr. Samuel Phillips of Tredrea.[2]

LAMORRAN
John and Catherine Verman 1658 1666
(Plate 23)

Arms: Gules, on a bend cotised Argent, 3 eagles displayed of the last.

Position: Against the south wall of the south transept.

Size: 8 feet by 4 feet.

Condition: Well preserved.

Style: Carved in low relief, the design is in the form of a border of strapwork, interspersed with eight shields of arms and a rose set in the two top corners. Placed within the border are two central arches, which frame the Latin inscriptions and epitaphs; and two smaller arches, all elaborately patterned and with winged angel heads between each. The arch on the left surmounts the figure of John Verman, kneeling on a cushion before a small pedestal on which is placed an open book. He wears his hair and beard cut in Stuart fashion and has a short cloak over his doublet. Above his head are carved rays, as of the sun, and above them some Hebrew letters.[3]

At the opposite end of the slate under a similar arch kneels Catherine Verman, his wife, wearing a wide-brimmed hat over a kerchief, a simple

---

[1] Wm. Greener, *Kilkhampton Church*, p. 19.
[2] Lake, Vol. II, p. 382.
[3] The Hebrew letters carved above the head of John Verman make up two words, Yahweh and Adoni, both Hebrew words for God. The former is the sacred, holy, unutterable word for God and the direct reading of the Hebrew letters is YHWH. No vowels were recorded in early Hebrew. Also note the fact that Hebrew is read from right to left (from the bottom of the page to the top) so these three consonants are HWYH. In addition there is a third character (rather like a question-mark) on the extreme right and two smaller markings above and below the second letter. As already stated, no Jew was allowed to utter the Holy name Yahweh although it was so written in manuscripts. To avoid the danger of accidentally reading aloud the holy and forbidden word, later scribes, after the introduction of vowels, added to the word Yahweh the vowels of the parmissable word Adoni. So, again reading from right to left are the vowel signs ADI (or ay). These then became part of the literary tradition and a permanent reminder that Adoni was to be read instead of Yahweh. Thus the word as it is carved on the memorial is in the form in which it is written in any Hebrew Testament.

LAMORRAN

Plate 23

Carved figures from the panel to John and Catherine Verman 1666

gown with a broad collar, and clasping between her hands a closed book. Some colour remains.

The eight shields displaying the family alliances are: Verman impaling Walrond; Verman impaling Coswarth; Verman quartering Penant; Verman quartering Trehane; Trehane quartering—; Trehane quartering Crocker; Trehane impaling Coswarth; Verman impaling Coswarth. At the lower edge of the slate is inscribed the name of the carver, Anthonius Colly Fecit & Scul.

> *Inscription:* Memoriae Sacrum. Hic Jacet Johannes Verman Dominus de Lamorran, et hujus Ecclesiae Patronus, qui obiit 21 die Janua. An'o D'oni 1658 et Aetatis Suae 71.
>
> Proxime sita est Chatherina Ejusdem Joh. Verman Uxor, quae Filia et Coheres Johanis Trehane de Trehane, Armig. Quae obiit 6 Die Martii, Anno Do'ni 1666 et an'o Aetatis Suae 67.[2]

John Verman was the second son of George Verman of Lamorran. He married Catherine, daughter and co-heiress of John Trehane of Trehane in Probus. By her he had four sons and three daughters of whom John, the eldest, married Mary, daughter of William Walrond of Bradfield in Devon. He died in 1658 aged 71 and his wife Catherine in 1666[3]

On the south side of the church, beyond the road, stands the remaining portion of the old manor house. Charles Henderson in his notes on the Parish of Lamorran says: " —Manor house (2 cottages) walls date from c.1600. Granite Tudor doorway in E. wall partially blocked now used as window. The door and 2 granite chimneys remain and their 16th century fireplaces are obscured by plaster. That on upper floor in excellent preservation. Cut on lintel initials J.V. (John Verman) with circular boss between. At South end of house small wing projects out upon the saltings or grassy mud flats covered at high tide. Possibly an entrance here accessible by boat. The plan of the house is interesting being unlike the usual Cornish dwelling of the early 17th century in ground plan."

Mary Verman 1665
(Plate 24)

Arms: Gules, on a bend cotised Argent, 3 eagles displayed of the last.

Position: Resting against the west wall of the south transept.

Size: 1 foot ten inches by 1 foot 7 inches.

Condition: Perfect.

Style: Framed in wood, this tablet, which is incised, has a decorated border surrounding the figure of a small girl reclining between a Latin inscription and epitaph. The arms of Verman and Walrond are each displayed on a lozenge. The child wears a bonnet and a full-skirted gown with laced bodice and wide collar. She rests her right elbow on a

---

[2] Complete epitaph Lake, Vol. II, p. 388—9.
[3] *Visitations C.*, p. 526.

Memoriæ dilectiſſimæ puella Mariæ filiæ
Joħ Verman Armig. quam ſuscepit primo
genitam ex Mariá uxore filia natu max
ima Guili. Walrond de Bradfield in Com Deu°
Armig Anunam efftavit Aug 29° 1665 Ætat 3°

Quem tulerat florem capuit mox terra fugaᵉᵐ
Vitæ principium quod tibi finis item
Matris delitæ vivens mortua Caeli
Pro gemma lapidem dat Superesse Deus

Plate 24   LAMORRAN
                          Mary Verman 1665

skull and crossed bones, and in her left hand she holds an hour-glass. Some trace of colour remains.

Inscription: Memoriae dilectissimae puella Mariae filiae Joh
 Verman Armig. quam fuscepit primo
  genitam ex Maria uxore filia natu max
  ima Guti. Walrond de Bradfield in Com. Devo.
  Armigr.Anunam efftavit Aug. 29.1665 Atat 3.
  Quem tulerat florem capuit mox terra fugacem
  Vitae principium quod tibi finis item
  Matris de litae vivens mortua Caeli
  Pro gemma lapidem dat Superesse Deus.

 Mary was the first-born child of John and Mary Verman. She died in 1665 at the age of three years.

LANDRAKE
Nicholas and Ebote Wills 1607
(Plate 25)

Arms: Argent, 3 wyverns passant in pale Sable, a bordure engrailed of the second bezantee.

Position: Two black slate panels set together against the south wall of the chancel inside the altar rail.[1]

Size: 5 feet 2 inches by 3 feet and 4 feet 6 inches by 3 feet.

Condition: Fairly good; formerly part of one large monument. The first panel has a very poorly cut and partly defaced verse at the top.

Style: The inscription and epitaph are framed by a border of vine decoration and an inset of strapwork design. At the bottom, against the floor, are two semi-circular pediments over the figures of a man and woman in an attitude of prayer, before open books. The man wears a ruff and his hair long, and the woman is in the traditional style gown with head-dress. At the top of the second panel is a large shield displaying the arms of Gifford. Below is a border inscription and set within it an angel's head carved in low relief; some lines of verse, and the figures of Death and an angel with labels of speech attached.

Inscription: That one in whome these two are one
  their names and blood in him so joyne,
  (herrin of both a lyving tombe,
  though of small proffe, Gaynst tymes to come)
  Their worth to right, his love to vent,
  Erected here this monument;
  though far behynde for cost and arte
  both his Desyer and their Desarte.

 Here lyeth the body of Nicholas Wylls, Gentleman, who departed this liefe the second Day of october 1607.

---

[1] A. J. Jewers, 1882, " Slate Slab Mural in north aisle."

LANDRAKE

Carved figures from the panel to Nicholas and Ebote Wills 1607

Plate 25

As Turtles true doe lyve and love together
In perfect blysse, durynge Each others lyefe;
Yett when the fates doe take Each one from other,
That one remaynes doth always pyne with Greife:
So these two Turtles that Intomb'd here lye
full many yeares, dyd pass in perfect love;
Tyll death dyd Sever theyre true sympathy,
To quite theyre loves with hevenly Joyes above.

G.W.

A Dying life after her death,
Deprived his spirits of vitall breath;
for his desire to seeke his mate,
hath Crown'd them both with Glorious state.

Heere lyeth the Body of Ebote, late wyfe unto Nycholas Wills
Gentleman. She Departed This lyfe & was Buryed the 19th
Day of June 1607

Deaths vizadge crime could not dismay
Her that in God did trust;
Although her body doe decaye,
Her soule rayneth with the just.
A corrupt body incorrupt shalbe;
A mortall crown'd with Immortallity.
a livinge death a dienge life,
hath freed her soule from worlds strife.

(Death) " Thou must away thy mortal body is but clay prepare
thyself " (Angel) " These bonds my soul lives in my Saviours
body. I am prepared dissolved."

Nicholas Wills of Smallacombe in St. Stephen-by-Saltash was one
of the eighteen children of Anthony Wills (by his first wife) of Pol-
drissick in Landrake. He married Ebbot, daughter of John Gifford,
and had 5 sons and 4 daughters.[2]

LANDULPH

FitzAntony Pennington 1768

(Plate 26)

Arms: Or, 5 lozenges in fess Azure.

Position: High up on the south wall inside the church tower.

Size: (Approx). 4 feet by 2 feet 6 inches.

Condition: Perfect.

Style: A headstone; at the top, carved in low relief, is the figure of
an angel in flight bearing in its right hand a trumpet and in the left
a bell.

[2] *Visitations C.*, p. 560.

Plate 26   LANDULPH
Carved figure from the tablet to Fitz Anthony Pennington 1768

Underneath is a four-lined verse and below that an incised drawing of an urn with fire issuing from its mouth symbolizing eternal life.

Inscription: Near this place lies the Body of FitzAntony Pennington, Bell-Founder, of the parish of Lezant in Cornwall who departed this life April 30.1768; Aetatis Suae 38.

> Tho' Boistrous Winds & Billows sore,
> Hath Tos'd me To and Fro;
> By God's Decree inspite of both,
> I Rest now here below.

This poor man had the misfortune to be caught in a storm, while crossing in a ferry-boat at Anthony with a new bell for Landulph. " The Penningtons of Cornwall were eminent and successful bellfounders. We find them residing at Bodmin as early as the reign of Queen Elizabeth. Robert Pennington of Bodmin had two sons, John and Bernard. John married and had seven sons, all baptised there, one of whom was probably the progenitor of the Penningtons of Lezant and Stoke Climsland, who carried on the business of bellfounders nominally at that place, but itinerating thence they cast their bells near the churches to which the bells belonged. Between 1702 and 1818 these popular founders cast nearly 500 bells in the county of Devon and, it is believed, as many in Cornwall. No pedigree of Pennington is recorded in the Heralds' Visitation of 1620 and the earliest evidence we have of the use of arms is a beautifully engraved seal attached to the will of Bernard Pennington of 1674."[1]

LANEAST

Roger Edgecombe 1677

Arms: Argent, an oak eradicated, crossed at the stem by a boar statant, both proper.

Position: Attached to the west wall of the north transept.

Condition: Fair. A carefully preserved fragment showing one corner of the border inscription and part of the epitaph. A drawing of this slate when complete was made by Sir Robert Edgecumbe, a direct descendant. A copy of it with an undated letter records the breaking of the slate when the church was restored.[2]

Style: A border inscription with fanciful capitals cut in relief. Inside the border are six lines of verse in script, between two panels of fruit and flower decoration carved in relief.

Inscription: Here lyeth the Body of Roger Edgecombe the younger of Tregeare who was buried the twenty fourth day of May 1677 Aetatis suoe 38.

[1] Maclean, Part I, Vol. I, p. 301.
[2] Henderson, E. Cornwall, Vol. p. 237.

The Wife's Valediction
Ah Love I little thought thou would'st have gone
And left me here behinde, thy death to mourne.
Thou wert more fit to take, the trouble rest,
And I the elder was first to have left.
But it hath pleased God that here I stay
And wait His time till I am called away.

Roger Edgecombe was the son of Roger Edgecombe and Jane Stroute of Egloskerry. By his wife Grace he had four sons and three daughters. In his will dated 18th May 1677[2] he gave to each of his six younger children the sum of two hundred pounds when they should accomplish the age of eighteen years.

The rest of his property he bequeathed to his wife and eldest son Roger.

The estate was partly in the parish of Laneast and partly in Egloskerry parish, with the old house at Tregeare (now replaced by a large Georgian residence) standing within the Egloskerry boundary.

From the inventory taken at the time of his death, it is apparent that Roger Edgcumbe was a well-to-do man and successful farmer. The sum of goods listed totals £1212 10s. 1d. quite a large sum by comparison with many of his contemporaries.

William Edgecumbe 1679

Position: Beside the memorial to Roger Edgecumbe.

Size: 2 feet 9 inches by 1 foot 11 inches.

Condition: Good.

Style: A border inscription in beautifully cut letters with some charming capitals and decorative scroll work, finely incised.

Inscription: Here lyeth the body of William the youngest sonne of
the sayd Roger Edgecumbe who was buryed the Twentieth day
of Decenber Anno Dom 1679 aetatis suce: 7 :

The Mother's Valediction
Deare Will: thou wert more like to live than I.
Longer, and yet I knew that thou must dye
My Benjamin: in bed: what shall I weep:
Noe, noe, I wont disturb thee of thy sleep:
Sleep on, I'le Joye, th'art freed from sin and payne:
Thought I the trouble have, thous reap'st ye gayne:

¹ C.R.O. wills.

F

Plate 27   LANIVET
John and Richard Courtney 1632

LANIVET
John and Richard Courtney 1559 1632
(Plate 27)

Arms: Or, 3 torteaux.

Position: Set low against the north wall.

Size: 5 feet 10 inches by 3 feet.

Condition: Very good.

Style: Carved in low relief is the three-quarter-length bearded figure of Richard Courtney, wearing a cloak over his doublet and knee breeches, and a wedding ring on his finger. He stands with clasped hands, between ornamented pilasters supporting an arch of five shields, which still bear traces of colour and the Courtney arms.

Below the figure is the inscription. This slate is very similar to that of Peter Bolt at Bodmin and may be the work of the same carver.

Inscription:

John ⎱ Courtney ⎰ Esqr. ⎱ was buried ye ⎰ first ⎱
Richard ⎰   ⎱ Gent. ⎰   ⎱ sixt ⎰

day of ⎰ March   1559
⎱ Dec'eber   1632

These liv'd and dyed both in Tremere;
God hath their souls, their bones lie here.
Richard with Thomsen his lovd wife,
Liv'd 61 yeeres, then ended lyfe.

John Courtney was the third son of Francis, of Ethy in St. Winnow, a younger branch of the Courtneys, Earls of Devon. He married Elizabeth daughter and co-heiress of Richard Trengove of Nance. John died young, leaving two daughters and three sons, of whom one, Richard the eldest, was but seven years old.

His widow then married Thomas Arundell of Lanherne, by whom she had a son Thomas, afterwards of St. Columb Major.

Richard Courtney married Thomazin, the eldest daughter of Nicholas Kendall of Pelyn in Lanlivery, and by her had one son William and three daughters; Joan, Loveday and Thomazin.[1]

Married at nineteen, Richard and Thomazin enjoyed an exceptionally long life together, until he died at the age of seventy-nine.

In his will he makes careful and loving provision for his wife, setting down the particular accommodation she is to enjoy in her son's house "... the chamber that I doe now lie in and the chamber over the little buttery to her proper use during her life with free ingress and egress for herself and her assigns." She was also to have a half share, during her life, of all the properties and lands of which Richard died possessed and was made joint executor of the will with her son William. Unlike many

---

[1] *Visitations C.*, p. 114—15.

of his contemporaries, Richard Courtney made his will four years before
his death, while in good health, ". . . I have written this my last will
with my own hand."[2]
Part of the old house still remains at Tremeer, on rising ground about
a mile north of the church. Succeeding generations have altered and
pulled down much of the original building. The last of the Courtneys
to live at Tremeer, Kelland Courtney and his wife Elizabeth, may have
put in the 18th Century south front as two ornamental lead drainheads
bear the initials K.C. and E.C.

LANLIVERY
Jane Kendall 1643
(Plate 28)

Arms: Argent, a chevron between 3 dolphins naint, embowed Sable.
Position: Set at floor level against the south wall of the Lady Chapel.
Size: 5 feet by 2 feet 7 inches.
Condition: Very good.
Style: The design of three arches springing from panelled supports
is set within a border of simple strap pattern with a rose in each top
corner. Beneath the centre arch is carved in low relief the youthful
figure of Jane Kendall, kneeling on a tasselled cushion before a pedestal
on which is placed an open book. Her simple dress has a falling lace-
edged collar and she wears a necklace and a loose hood over her curls.
A label issues from her mouth. " My Spirit doth heaven inherit."
Under the left-hand arch is a shield bearing the arms of Kendall; and
the third arch frames the inscription tablet.
This slate was probably the backplate of a tomb-chest as the border
pattern is on three sides only. Writing in 1882 J. A. Jewers describes
this slate as a floorslab.
Inscription: Here lyeth the Body of Jane the Daughter of
Nicholas Kendall of Pelyn Esq. who was Buried the 20th of
January Anno Dommini 1643.
Jane was the only daughter and the eldest of the six children of
Nicholas and Emline Kendall. She died at the age of nineteen, about
three years after her father's death.[1] Pelyn, which has been the home of
the Kendall family for more than four centuries, lies in a pleasant
wooded valley, about a mile south of the church. Built on the E plan,
the two lateral wings are the oldest parts of the house remaining.
A granite doorway in the east wing bears the initials I K (John Kendall)
and W K (Walter Kendall) with the date 1660.
The family was originally called de Kendall and Sir John de Kendall
had the custody of Restormel Castle under Edward the Black Prince.
The family are still in residence and represented by Nicholas Kendall
Esq., High Sheriff in 1960.

[2] C.R.O. wills.
[1] *Visitations C.*, p. 260.

My Spirit
doth heauen
Inherit

Here lyeth the
Body of Jane the
Daughter of Nich:
olas Kendall of
Pelyn Eſq who
was Buried the
20ᵗʰ of January
Anno Dommini
1643

LANLIVERY
Jane Kendall 1643

Plate 28

LANREATH
Sir John and Lady Grace Grylls 1649 1653

Arms: Or, 3 Bendlets enhanced Gules.

Position: Fixed high up on the south wall of the Lady Chapel.

Condition: Very good. Coloured.

Style: Well cut and set within a wooden frame, above which is carved a porcupine, are the crest and arms of Grylls quartering Bere. On the left side is an inscription to Sir John Grylls and on the right side, one to his wife.

Inscription: In memory of Sr John Grylls, Kt. who was Buried the 30th day of December, Anno Domi 1649. As also of the Lady Grace his wife, who was inter'd the 19th of Nove'ber 1653: This tomb was erected by their Sone & heire Charles in 1666.

Sir John was the eldest son of Charles Grylls, Councillor at Law, of Court in Lanreath, and Agnes daughter of George Stubb Esq., of Trengoff. He married Grace, the eldest daughter and co-heiress of William Bere of St. Neot[1] and had four sons and four daughters. He became High Sheriff in 1641 and was knighted on the field of battle by Charles I.[2] In 1623 he erected the unique wooden monument in the chancel of Lanreath church, to the memory of his father and mother and five of their children.

Court is situated close by the church and remains for the most part very much the charming Tudor house built about 1612.

LANSALLOS
Margery Budockshide 1579
(Plate 29)

Arms: Sable, 3 lozenges in fess between as many stags heads cabossed, Argent.

Position: Fixed to the wall of the south aisle.

Size: 5 feet 4 inches by 24—30 inches. Coffin-shaped panel.

Condition: Poor. Broken apart and repaired; probably when removed from chancel floor during restoration work.[3] Figure worn smooth.

Style: Inside a narrow border with a Latin inscription, is carved in relief the full-length figure of a woman wearing a tall-crowned hat with her ruff and brocaded gown. In her right hand she carries a pair of gloves and in her left a prayerbook. There are two shields behind her head displaying Smith impaling " a buck trippant "; and Smith impaling Budockshide. In the space between her feet is the carver's signature " per peteur croker fecit."

---

[1] Slate monument at St. Neot.
[2] Lake, Vol. III, p. 36.
[3] Church notes for visitors.

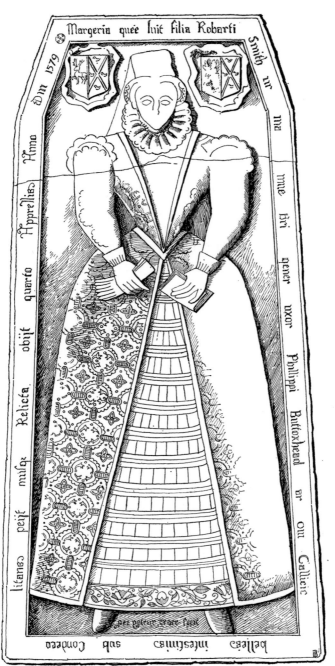

Plate 29   LANSALLOS
Margery Budockshide 1579

Inscription: Margeria quee suit filia Roberti Smith ... ur ... ma
... mue (B)ri ... gener uxor Phillippi Buttoxhead ... ar om
Gallici ... belles intestinis ... sub Condeeo ... litans peijt
mus ... Relicta obijt quarto Apprellis Dm 1579.

Margery Budockshide, spelt " Buttoxhead " on the monument, was
a daughter of Robert Smith of Tregonick in St. Germans and sister to
John Smith of Duloe.[4] The identity of her first husband is not known,
as the name on the monument is defaced, although his impalement of
arms " a buck trippant " is quite clear.   Her second husband was
Phillip Budockshide, son and heir of Roger Budockshide of St. Budeaux.
He spent much of his time fighting overseas and died in 1570 in France.[5]
Margery Budockshide died in 1579.

LANTEGLOS-BY-FOWEY

Thomas Beale 1645

Position: Fixed to the wall of the south aisle.

Size: 5 feet 2 inches by 2 feet 3 inches.

Condition: Good.

Style: Rather crudely carved, the inscription and verse are set side by
side within a quaintly incised pattern of tulips.   The flowers on three
sides are half open, and the rest full-blown.

Inscription: Thomas Beale of Churchtowne yeoman was buried
the 4th day of February Anno Domini 1645 Being about the
age of 85 yeares.
Of earth Gods wisedome made me
on earth Gods love did please me
To earth Gods Justice domed me
From earth Gods power shall raise me
And earth if any will, Ile not complaine one thee
that hast, art, wilt be such a friend to me.
Death is to me advantage.

In his will dated the 19th day of March 1638[1] and seven years before
his death, Thomas Beale bequeathed various items of furniture and
token gifts of money to each of his six married daughters.   To Mary,
his unmarried daughter, he gave one hundred pounds, provided she
married with her mother's consent.   The fourth daughter, Julian, and
her husband, Michael Gully, inherited the estate at Tremeer; paying
the widow £20 yearly and allowing her one chamber above the parlour.
Tremeer lies about two miles north-east from the church.

---

[4] *Visitations C.*, p. 427.
[5] A. L. Rowse, *Sir Richard Grenville*, p. 62—3.
[1] C.R.O.

John Mayow 1645

Arms: Gules, a chevron vair between 3 ducal coronets Or.

Position: Fixed to the sill of a window in the north wall.

Condition: A soft slate, rather worn.

Style: On the slate are cut the arms and crest of Mayow and six lines of interesting verse.

Inscription: To the memory of John Mayow, of Polruan, Gent., who departed this life the 28 of Decem'r, in the yeare of our Lord 1645.

> Loe here a Marchant who both lost and gott,
> by sea and land; such was his various lot;
> but never lost he less, nor gott he more
> then when he left earth, sea, for heaven's shore
> who lives at peace with God, and faithful dies
> out lives all stormes, and in God's bosom lies.

LELANT

William Praed 1620

(*Plate 30*)

Arms: Per pale indented Sable and Ermine, on a chevron Gules 5 cross patee Or.

Position: Well set against the west wall of the south aisle.

Size: 6 feet by 3 feet.

is suffered severe flaking as if

rved in relief an elongated arch iam Praed, his wife and four n wears a gown with hanging versized thimble-crowned hat, igures are very plainly dressed ie son and third daughter are : each figure. Two decorated ier of a skull and hour-glass,

CORRIGENDUM

P. 81. Arms of Praed should read Azure 6 mullets in pile Argent

Those in the text are of Mackworth with whom the Praed arms were quartered from 1717.

...... the boaye of William Praed of Trevethow Gentleman of the adge of five and fiftye yeeres who was Buried the Eight of maye anno dni.1620 having one sone and three daughters surviving.

> Think gentle friend, that now dost view this tomb,
> Tomorrow must thou go to thy last home.

It is curious that a man of some property and social standing, such as James Praed, did not employ the services of a skilled carver when setting up this monument to his father.

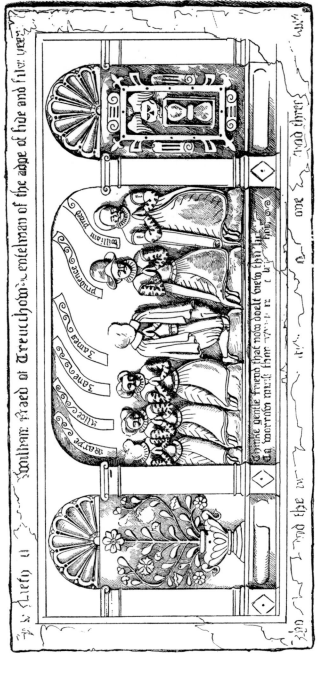

Plate 30

LELANT
William Praed 1624

William Praed, son of James Praed of Trevethow, was born in 1565 and married Prudence, the youngest child of Stephen Pawley of Gunwin in Lelant, by whom he had two sons and four daughters.[1] His wife and two elder children predeceased him and Jane (the fourth figure on the slate) was married to John Coode of Sethnoe in Breage, and died in 1626 aged 30.[2] In his will dated 6th April 1620,[3] a month before his death, he bequeathed the sum of £300 to each of his two daughters, Alice and Mary, upon their attaining the age of 21 years or at their marriage. He directed his son James, as executor, to provide " Diet, lodging apparell and necessaries for them until their portion is due." His nephew called " my Cosen Hewgh Pawley " was given £3 6s. 8d. lawful money; and the rest of his goods and estate he bequeathed to his son James aged twenty-four at the time of his father's death.

The inventory of goods attached to the will contains several entries of interest, namely:

In the Parlour—1 threedturne (=spinning wheel)
In the Haule—the sylinge (=the tapestry)
In the Buttery—a voider (=basket for bones or remains of a meal)

The Chamber over the Buttery was evidently William Praed's own room and contained the following items:

One stead bed furnished	
three chests one desk one sideboard and one case to hold bottles	£7.0.0
two pair of holland sheets	£2.10.0
one holbert one bowe	
one close stool and one other little stool	9.0
In the desk one gold ring, three silver seals and three dozen of silver buttons	£4
one silk skarffe	13.4
a cupboard of boxes to hold writings	15.0
four suits of apparell, one nightgown two cloaks two hats with the rest of his wearing apparell	£16.10.0
his books	£20.0.0

The Lelant Subsidy list of 1641 commences with the name of James Praed Gent., but in 1664 he is described as esquire. James Praed Esq., whose estate was valued at £600 per annum, was Sheriff for the county under the Commonwealth in 1654 and elected M.P. for St. Ives in 1661.[4]

Trevethow is most pleasantly situated about one mile south of the church and overlooking the Hayle estuary. The house was largely rebuilt in 1761 by Humphrey Mackworth-Praed Esq.

[1] G. C. Boase, *Collectanea Cornubiensia*, p. 755.
[2] Wooden monument at Breage.
[3] C.R.O.
[4] J. H. Matthews, *History of St. Ives, Lelant, Towednack and Zennor*, 1892, p. 198, 203.

LELANT
Stephen Pawley 1635

Plate 31

Stephen Pawley 1635

(Plate 31)

Arms: Or, a lion rampant Sable on a chief dauncette of the second, 3 mullets Argent.

Position: Fixed to the west wall of the south aisle.

Size: 6 feet by 3 feet.

Condition: Very worn. A soft light-grey slate flaking badly.

Style: Inside a border inscription cut in low relief are the figures of Stephen Pawley, his wife, five sons and six daughters. The man, wearing doublet and trunks beneath a travelling cloak, kneels beside a prayer stool. His wife, with a tall-crowned hat and clasping a closed book kneels at his side. Between them is a shield bearing the arms of Pawley impaling Tresteane. A second shield shows the same arms quarterly. Only the three eldest sons and their father kneel on cushions. Over the head of each child and the mother are set their initials. Below the figures is the remnant of an eight-lined verse, formerly concealed by water pipes.

Inscription: Here lyeth the Bodye of Stephen Pawley of this Parish Gentleman who dyed the XIX daye of November in ye yeare of our Lord God 1635.

If teares the dead againe to life could calle
Thou hadst not slept within this earthye balle
If holye vertues could a ransome bynn
Soe soone corruption had not rapte thee in
But thou wert ripe for God and God didst crave
Soe gavst a gladsome welcome to the grave
Assuringe still that thou with God dost dwell
Thy end soe good thy life was lead soe well.

Stephen Pawley was the eldest of the nine children of Stephen and Jane Pawley of Gunwin, and brother to Prudence who married William Praed. He married Margery, daughter and heir of Robert Tresteane of Veryan, and by her had five sons and six daughters. The fourth son Robert married Ann, daughter of Mr. Purfoy of St. Ives. Jane, the eldest daughter, married J. Ustick; Margery, the second daughter, married John South; Grace, fifth daughter, married David Mathew of Glamorgan; Prudence, sixth daughter, married E. Polkinghorne; and Cheston married John Borlase of Pendeen.[5]

This family was anciently seated at Gunwin in Lelant. In the Subsidy of 1327 " Johannes Paly " is rated at £2 10s. 0d. by the year. In the same roll " Stephanus Pawlye " is named as possessing goods at Lelant of the annual value of £20. In 1523, Stephen Pawley's goods at

---

[5] *Collectanea Cornubiensia,* p. 755.

Lelant were worth £20 a year; and Radulph the servant of Stephen
Pawly, was in receipt of £1 annual wages. In 1629, Stephen Pawly in
goods £3.[6] The family fortunes continued to decline and the eldest male
line became extinct on the death of Hugh Pawley in 1724. Junior
branches survived for several generations. The last survivor, Miss Jane
Pawley, died in poverty.

Judith and Hugh Pawley 1698 1721

Position: In a shallow recess, west wall of south aisle.

Size: 6 feet 9 inches by 3 feet 2 inches.

Condition: Perfect. A handsome marble slate.

Style: The crest and arms of Pawley quartered with Tresteane and
(Renfry?)[7] Below is the inscription set out in good Roman lettering.

Inscription: Fili Dei miserare nobis
                Miseris Peccatoribus
This Marble Stone was placed here in the year of our Lord
1713 In Memory of Hugh Pawley of Gunwin Gent. who dyed
the 17th day of September Anno 1721 & of Judith his wife who
dyed ye 30th day of October 1698 by whom were begotten
seaven children (viz) Prudence, Hugh, Mary, William, George,
Peter, & Judith.
                Virtus post Funera Vivit
                Vita quasi umbra fugit.

The date 1713 on this slate would seem to be a mistake and should
perhaps read 1723. In his will dated 25th July 1721,[8] Hugh Pawley
(grandson of Stephen) names each of his four surviving children,
Prudence, Hugh, Mary and William. To Prudence ". . . my dearly
beloved daughter who has been so extreamly serviceable and dutyfull
unto me all her lifetime—all my money Gold and Silver . . . all my
Gold Locketts sett with stones and Gold chains and Rings . . . the
Table looking glasses . . . one silver Tankard and silver salver being the
last of the Two I owne." He also bequeathed to her his lands at
Porthminster, the Warren and sands, the Ropewalk, and at Penolver and
the right to " Digg Delve Search and look for tyn . . ." His eldest son,
Hugh, inherited the lease of " Pullsulesack (Pulsack) and Parkan-
noweth " in Phillack parish. The ultimate inheritor of all the estates
and the sole executor of the will was to be his grandson William Pawley.

Gunwin lies near the cliffs about a mile north-west from the church.
It was rebuilt as a farmhouse during the late 19th century.

⁶ J. H. Matthews, *A History of St. Ives, Lelant, Towednack and Zennor*, p. 200.
⁷ *Cornubiensia*, p. 666.
⁸ C.R.O.

LEZANT

Thomas Trefusis 1606

(Plate 32)

Arms: Argent, a chevron between 3 spindles Sable, a crescent for difference.

Position: Standing in the south-east corner of the south aisle.

Size: 5 feet 8 inches by 5 feet.

Condition: Fair.

Style: This memorial is made up of a chest with backplate and end wall-panel. Carved in relief on the backplate, inside a border pattern of strapwork, are three shields. The first shield displays the arms of Trefusis quartered with Tresithney; the centre shield shows the crest and arms of Trefusis impaling Coryton; and on the third shield the arms of Trefusis quartering Milliton. Some slight traces of colour remain.

At a right-angle against the south wall is a panel, measuring 2 feet 11 inches by 2 feet 2 inches, divided into two parts by a border showing an angel's head and a pattern of trailing vine. In the top half is the figure of Thomas Trefusis kneeling on a cushion before a prayer pedestal with an open book on it. He wears a ruff with his doublet and trunk-hose, and behind him his wife kneels wearing traditional gown and head-dress. On the lower half of the panel are carved the kneeling figures of two sons and two daughters, the second daughter already deceased, as shown by a small skull.

On the top panel of the chest, which is badly cracked and worn, are two verses, one of them in Latin.

The front panel is decorated with a design of four scrolls each with a Latin phrase.

The end panel has a verse and simple incised pattern.

This monument has the appearance of having been made up of two separate tombs. The chest itself is of a different slate and size from the back, top and figured panels.

Inscription:

> This marble monument faiere though it be,
> Trefusis, yet is farre unfit for thee;
> Unfit, because unlike this hard heyune stone,
> Thou meek and mild, incidious unto none;
> This base as beynge, if traced out of earth;
> Thou generous by descent, of ancient birth;
> And which is most, this fraile and ever wastinge;
> But thou eternall now and ever lastinge.
> Only herein this tomb seems like to thee,
> As this, so thou in Church still lovest to bee.
> The soules of those whose bodies thus ar spent,
> seated above the starry firmament,

Plate 32 LEZANT
Thomas Trefusis 1606

have gaynd astate more permanent and sure;
let him (that hopes to have his howse indure
for ever) build it there, where death nor fate
shall alter or determine his estate.

Thomas Trefusis was the son and heir of Nicholas Trefusis of
Landew and his wife Grace, daughter and co-heiress of William
Milliton of Pengersick. He married Mary the eldest daughter of Peter
Coryton of West Newton and had two sons Nicholas and William, and
two daughters of whom only Mary survived. He was a grandson of
Thomas Trefusis of Trefusis by his second wife Melior Tresithney.[1]

In his will dated 3rd February 1606[2] Thomas wrote ". . . I give my
sonne Nicholas my baye Mare and my little nagge. Item I give him my
Rynge of goulde wherewith I seale and myne Armoure and furniture
for the Warres."

Among the many bequests to his wife he includes, ". . . I give her a
chayne of gould and the rest of her Jewells which she hathe, . . . and my
will is that my wife shall have the custodie keeping governing and
bringing up of my eldest sonne and of his goods and lands untill he be
of the age of one and twentie yeres and so likewise of my youngest sonne
and of my daughter and her portion likewise (except they be before
marryed)."

Nicholas Trefusis Esq., son and heir of Thomas, was aged eighteen
years when his father died in 1610. He married in 1615 Katharine
daughter of John Lampen of Padreda in Linkinhorne and by her had
two daughters.[3]

In 1627 he was one of three Cornish gentlemen struck off the
Commission of the Peace for refusing to contribute to the Forced Loan
of Charles I. During the Civil War he was active as a Parliamentarian
and in 1646 was elected a Knight of the Shire. In 1648, however, he was
secluded from the House of Commons by Prides Purge, along with some
hundred Presbyterian members, for refusing to sit in judgement on
the King.[4]

Mary Trefusis married Robert Rashleigh of Fowey. Katharine
Trefusis married Richard Killowe, of Roselyon in St. Blazey.

Landew is situated on well wooded, rising ground about a mile north-
east from the church. Thomas Trefusis acquired Landew in 1582 and
it continued in the family until the death of Nicholas, when it passed to
his daughter Mary, the wife of Edward Herle and their heirs.

---

[1] *Visitations C.*, p. 567.
[2] P.C.C. wills.
[3] *Visitations C.*, p. 567.
[4] Mary Coate, *Cornwall in the Great Civil War*, p. 20, 244.

G

LISKEARD

Thomas Johnson 1666

Arms: A chevron between 3 lions heads erased, crowned.

Position: Set against the wall behind the chancel altar.

Condition: Excellent. Good lettering.

Style: A large slate slab which is divided into two panels (possibly two slabs originally) one showing a shield with the arms of Johnson impaling Morton. On the other panel the same arms are repeated on a widow's lozenge.

Inscription: In May 1666 was here interred ye Body of Thomas Johnson aged 57 who was Major in ye Duke of Albermarles Regiment of horse and a Coldstreamer he was Son & heir of John Johnson of Bark by Thorpe in ye County of Leicester. Gent. In August 1688 here was interred ye Body of Elizabeth ye widdow of ye said Major Johnson aged 67 she was ye Eldest Daughter of John Morton of Syleby in ye County of Leicester Esq.

Thomas Johnson was born at Barkly Thorpe near Leicester in 1609. He had been an officer in the Parliamentary Army and became Major under General Monk. In 1651, he purchased of the Parliament the Duchy Manor of Lodge or Liskeard Park for £3,500, one half of the amount being allowed him in debentures, probably for his own services. He was a leading Presbyterian at Liskeard.[1]

Mary Read 1731

Position: Fixed to the east wall of the Lady Chapel, outside.

Size: 2 feet 7 inches by 1 foot 5 inches.

Condition: Good.

Style: The very crude inscription is set within an oval, and an angel's head is carved at the bottom. In each corner at the top of the slate is an angel's head, and in the two bottom corners are the small figures of a girl, one kneeling and the other standing.

Inscription: Mary Read. Junior of this burrough obiit Quintus Des Novembris 1731 Aetatis Suae Viginti Tertius or 23.

Epitaph
Under a maiden meek & Chast
prud'nt & just through devine grace
youthes blosoms nept by pain Opprest
Now Joyned wt Saints her flesh to rest
Till ye resurrection of the Just

[1] J. Allen, *History of Liskeard*, p. 321.

Sights & Tears All Greves now flee
Ar by Christ Changd for Endlis Joy
Chanting wt ye Celestiall Quyir onhig
To Laud & prise ye Glorious Trinity
wt Cherubins Above ye sky
Sec Lucam 10th. V. 42.
Atquiuno, opus, est Et Maria vero bonam Partem Elegit quae
non ausretur ab Ei Quae et Resurrectienem ei Corpus cy vitam
aeternam Aylic

LUDGVAN

John South 1636

(Plate 33)

Position: Attached to the north wall of the chancel, inside the altar
rail; formerly on the sill of the east window.

Size: 4 feet by 2 feet 6 inches.

Condition: Fair but rather worn. Soft light-grey slate.

Style: Crudely carved within a border inscription are the full-length
figures of John South and his wife Margery with their five children
kneeling beside them, two sons and three daughters. The man wears
a ruff and robe with hanging sleeves. Beside him is a closed book on a
prayer stool and above it a shield of arms, defaced. His wife holds a
closed book and wears a ruff and hat with her simple gown. Of the five
children, only four are named in the Ludgvan register of baptisms,
they are: John, Oct. 26th 1629; William, April 26th 1632; Mary,
May 24th 1628 and Blanch, Nov. 20th 1634. The figures are very worn
and most of the features are quite gone. Below is cut an unusual eight-
lined verse.

Inscription: Here Lyeth the Body of John South Mr of Arts who
died Rector of this Parish ye 6th Daye of October in the year of
our Lord God 1636.

Let Natures courter Children have
A Tonguelesse Tombe, or but a grave
South the meridian point of wit
Can never set but shine in it
Ripe artist, and divine inspird
Thou liv'dst, Thou di'dst, beloved admird
Hyperbolize I doe not: True
All's here Dear Dearest friend adue.

John South was vicar of Lelant from 1624 to 1631 and rector of
Ludgvan until his death in 1636.[1]

[1] According to G. C. Boase's *Collectanea Cornubiensia* he married Margery, the second daughter
of Stephen Pawley of Lelant and she, after the death of her husband, married Thomas Corey who
succeeded him at Lelant. This statement however must be discredited as the impalement of
arms carved on the slate, although defaced, is not that of Pawley.

LUDGVAN
John South 1631

Plate 33

An undated Terrier for Ludgvan[2] provides an interesting account of the church furnishings during John South's incumbency:
A note what goods the prish hath
Two Sarples one with sleeves for the minister and one without sleeves for the Clarke.
Two bookes of common prayer
one bibell of the new translation
The works of bishop Jewell
The booke of homilies
The booke of Cannons.
One Carpet for the Lords table & a linnen cloth for the Lords Table
one Silver Cupp for to hould the wine ppared for the Lords Table & an other peece of plate for to hould the breade
fower linnen cloths for the deaske
six linnen clothes for the fonte
one Pulpit Cloth.   Joh. South Rector ibid

William Trevoran ⎫   James (Gw)avas ⎫
                 ⎬ Churchwardens   ⎬ sidmen
Henry Steven   ⎭   Richard Edwards ⎭

MADRON
Thomas Fleming 1631
Thomas and Alice Cock 1601 1610
(Plate 34)

Arms: Fleming:—Vaire, a chief chequy Or and Gules
        Cock:—Lozengy, on a fess 3 cocks proper
Position: Fixed to the east wall of the Lady Chapel.
Size: 6 feet 6 inches by 3 feet.
Condition: Excellent. Re-cut in recent years by a local carver.[1]
Style: Inside a border inscription are the incised figures of Thomas Cock and his wife Alice, standing side by side with a shield between them displaying the arms of Cock impaling—. The man is plainly dressed in a ruff, doublet and breeches. The woman wears a simple gown and small hat. Below them are the full-length figures of Thomas Fleming and his wife Elizabeth with the arms of Fleming and Cock on a shield between them. The man has a more elaborate doublet and wears an ornamented purse and short sword scabbard at his left side. Set at his right side is a Justice's staff. The woman wears a quilted petticoat with her gown and a small brimmed hat. She holds an open book. Below these two figures are carved their ten children, all kneeling the sons with clasped hands and the daughters alternately with hands folded and clasped. The initials are cut beside each figure.

[2] C.R.O.
[1] Arnold Snell of Newlyn.

Plate 34   MADRON
Thomas Fleming, Thomas and Alice Cock 1631

Inscription: Here lyeth ye Bodyes of Thomas Fleming Gent who was buried ye 14th day of June 1631. Thomas Cock Gent was buried ye 9th Day of December 1601. Alice his wife was buried ye 5 day of January 1610.

On the adjoining wall is a tablet of slate with the following inscription and measuring 2 feet 6 inches by 2 feet 5 inches:—

An Epitaph to ye memorye of ye disceased Thomas Fleming Gent.

Fleming ye ayde to neighbours poore opprest,
interred here beneath that tomb doth rest.
His wydowes teres nor phisicks helpe could save,
nor childrens cries, his body from ye grave.
But that from greved hearts the sigh and saye,
lamentinge oft, they wante their only staye.
His sonnis and daughters and his wife withal
even syde by syde doe with one funerall.
His neighbours, soldiers, kinsman, and ech one,
doe deck his herse with sadness mourneful mone;
Sayinge hees gone whome we must needs commend,
a true peace maker and faithful friend.
Beloved of all not hated once whose pure
and good report for ever shall endure.
Concludinge thus his soule to heaven did fly;
that well did live and ended gloriously.

The Flemings first came from Munster, in Ireland, to Bristol and were later given Landithy by the Crown. The father of Thomas was Nicholas, whose eldest son was John, Warden of Wadham College Oxford and chaplain to James I.

Thomas married Elizabeth, daughter and heiress of Thomas Cock (of Bodmin) by whom he had three sons and seven daughters:[2] Nicholas bap. 1601, married Ann, daughter of John Clies, second Mayor of Penzance, in 1631 upon inheriting Landithy. Thomas bap. 1604, married Mary Harris of Kenegie. John bap. 1622. Frances—. Grace bap. 1602, married Richard Angwin 1646. Ann bap. 1606. Elizabeth bap. 1608, married John Keate, vicar of Madron 1627—1647. Mary bap. 1610, married Robert Colman 1636. Phillippa bap. 1611. Jane bap. 1616 married Thomas Chirgwin 1656.

The Flemings held for a time both the Advowson and the rectorial tithe. Landithy was given to the Knights of St. John by Henry de Pomeroy in the 12th century and was held by them until their order was suppressed in 1540. It was then held by the Crown until Queen Elizabeth granted it to Nicholas Fleming.[3] Landithy is now a farm opposite the church, with scarcely a trace of the old house remaining.

[2] *Visitations C.*, p. 164.
[3] H. R. Jennings, *Historical Notes on Madron Morvah and Penzance*, 1936.

MADRON
John Maddern 1621

Plate 35

John Maddern 1621

(*Plate 35*)

Position: Attached to the wall of the south aisle.

Size: 6 feet by 3 feet.

Condition: Excellent; re-cut at the same time as the Fleming slate.

Style: Set within a border inscription are the incised figures of a man and woman, separated from the epitaph by a pilaster ornamented with three roses. The man, wearing doublet and breeches, kneels on a small cushion beside a prayer stool on which is a closed book. Above is the date 1595 and a shield displaying a chevron ermine.

Beside him, his wife also kneels on a cushion, wearing the traditional gown and ruff of the period with a thimble-crowned hat and clasping a closed book. Between the two figures is a shield displaying the arms of Trevanion; on a fess between two chevrons, three escallops. A third shield shows: on a chevron between three stags (?) three mullets. The drawing is crude but the lettering good.

Inscription: Here lieth the Body of John the sonne of John Maddern, Gentleman, who departed this life in the feare of God the — day of August, Anno Domini 1621:

> If teares the dead againe to life could call
> thou hadst not slept with in this earthly ball
> If holy vertues could aransome bine
> Soe sone corrupcion had not wrapt thee in
> But thou were ripe for god and god didst crave
> Soe gavest a gladsome wellcombe to the grave
> Assuring still that thou with god dost dwell
> Thy end soe good thy life was lead so well.
> Aetatis Sue 1595. Aetatis Sue 25.

John Cossen, alias Maddern,[4] descended from Maderne Cossen and eldest son of John Maddern and Anne Trevanion. He married Anne, daughter of John Guavis of Sithney in 1620 and died within the year without issue.[5]

---

[4] Although the first Mayor of Penzance was a John Maddern he could not have been (as is generally stated) the young man carved on the slate, for he was aged only eighteen when the charter was granted in 1614.

[5] *Visitations C.*, p. 103.

Plate 36   ST. MARTIN-BY-LOOE
Carved figure from the tomb of Philip Mayowe 1590

ST. MARTIN-BY-LOOE

Phillip Mayowe 1590

(Plate 36)

Arms: Gules, a chevron vair between three ducal coronets Or.

Position: On the south side of the chancel and inside the altar rail. A ledger stone set on a concrete chest, in an arched recess. Formerly on the floor of the Sanctuary.

Size: 6 feet 3 inches by 2 feet 9 inches.

Condition: Good, except for the wearing away of some of the pattern on the robe of the figure.

Style: Inside a border inscription is carved, in bold relief, the full length figure of a man wearing a ruff with a richly patterned fur-trimmed robe. His head rests on a large embroidered cushion. Against the wall is a backplate on which the crude figures of Adam and Eve are carved; each holding a skull and a branch of fruiting vine. In the centre is a decorated arch supported on pilasters and under it a shield displaying the arms of Mayowe impaling those of the Merchant Adventurers Company. Eight lines of verse complete the design.

Inscription: Here lyeth the Bodye of Phillipe Maiowe, of East Looe, Gentleman, who deceased this lyfe the XXIIII daye of August in the yeare 1590: being then of the age of LXXII yeares.

> Here under this great carved stone
> is phillipe Maiow entombde;
> who in his life for merchandice
> Was through this lande renown'd
> His trade was great, his dealins just,
> the poor did feele his bountie.
> Great cost he put for sea and land
> in buildyng verye plentie.

Phillip Mayowe was the son of Phillip Mayowe and Margaret Smith. He married a daughter of — Webb of Tavistock and by her had one son, John, who pre-deceased him; and a daughter, Margery.[1] In his will dated 7th August 1590[2] he gave " towards the repairing of Loowe Bridge twentie shillings Currente monye of Englande and towards the reliffe of the poore people in East Loowe another twentie shillings of like good money." To each of his six grandchildren he left gifts of money and the eldest, Phillip, he named as his heir and executor.

---

[1] *Visitations C.*, p. 315.
[2] C.R.O. wills.

Here lyeth ÿ Bodye

eturlia

uﬀead morum
Vitæ.

of Henry Stephen Gentleman and of Dorothy his wife in certen

Glorious resurrection which God of his Mercy graunt

Hope ÿ expectation of a

He died ÿ 11 of February
1611 Shee died ÿ 24 of
July 1630 This Memori
was erected by JohnFrauncis
Dorothy their 11 children

Plate 37   St. Mawgan-in-Pydar
Henry and Dorothy Stephen 1630

ST. MAWGAN-IN-PYDER

Henry and Dorothy Stephen 1611 1630

(Plate 37)

Position: Set against the west wall of the nave.

Size: 5 feet 11 inches by 2 feet 8 inches.

Condition: Fair

Style: Within a border inscription are carved, in low relief, the full-length figures of Henry Stephen and his wife Dorothy. The proportions of the figures, particularly that of the man, are very crude. He wears a ruff, tunic and breeches with fancy knee-bands. The woman has on a small-crowned hat and simply styled full-skirted dress. At the top of the slate is a partly obliterated Latin inscription and at the bottom the dates of death.

Inscription: Here lyeth ye Bodye of Henry Stephen Gentleman and of Dorothy his wife in certen hope & expectation of a Glorious resurrection which God of his Mercy graunt.
He died ye 11 of February 1611 Shee died ye 24 of July 1630 This Memori was erected by John Frauncis Dorothy their 11 children.

MENHENIOT

John Trelawny 1563

Arms: A chevron Sable between 3 oakleaves proper.

Position: Attached to the wall of the south aisle.

Size: 2 feet 6 inches by 5 feet.

Condition: Perfect.

Style: A semi-circular slate plate, probably part of a dismantled tomb. Carved in bold relief are the coarsely drawn figures of two putti supporting a shield of six quarterings: Trelawny; Pincerna; Courtney (2); in a border 12 fleur-de-lys; and Lamellion. Beneath the shield are the letters IT. This slate is so much like the Tredeneck monument at St. Breock, in both workmanship and design, that it should be accepted as by the same carver.

John Trelawny of Pool was the son and heir of Walter Trelawny. He was M.P. for Liskeard in 1552—3 and married first, Margery Lamellion by whom he had one son. His second wife was Lora Trecarrel and she bore him two sons. He died in 1563.[1]

Pool was situated on low ground to the south of the church.

[1] *Visitations C.*, p. 576.

MEVAGISSEY
Lewis Dart 1632

Plate 38

MEVAGISSEY

Lewis Dart 1632

(Plate 38)

Arms: Gules, a fess and canton Ermine.

Position: Cemented to the north wall of the aisle.

Size: 4 feet by 2 feet.

Condition: Perfect.

Style: Crudely carved in low relief, are the kneeling figures of Lewis Dart, his wife Elizabeth and their eight children, set beneath two arches supported by three ornamented pilasters. On the left side the man, in armour, kneels upon an embroidered cushion and beside him is a staff in the form of a dart. Behind him are his six sons; the three eldest kneel on cushions and are bearded like their father; all are dressed in doublet and knee breeches.

On the right-hand side the woman also kneels upon an embroidered cushion. She wears the traditional head-dress with a ruff and quilted gown; beside her is carved a fleur-de-lys. Kneeling behind her are two daughters, each on a smaller cushion and wearing the simple caps, ruffs and gowns of the period. In the top left-hand corner of the slate is a shield displaying the arms of Dart impaled.[1] In the centre is a second shield with the arms of Dart impaling Roscarrock and in the right-hand corner the arms of Roscarrock. The inscription is set above the heads of the figures and a quaint rhyming epitaph occupies the base of the design.

Inscription: Heere lyeth the bodye of Lewis Dart of Pentuwen esquire who was buried the XIIth day of Aprill Anno Domini 1632 which maried Elizabeath daughter of Thomas Roscarrocke esquire & hade issue VI sonnes & 2 daughters.

> Death shoots sometimes as archers doe
> one darte to finde another
> But now by shooting 'thath founde foure
> and all layd hear together.[2]
> Here lyes the father & his sonnes
> foure darts whose name shall bee
> (although their dayes on earth be donne)
> praysed to eternitye.
> The warfar past the darts must rest
> This grave shall be the quiver
> where they shall rest till with ye ble
> they be reviv'd for ever.

---

[1] Ancient arms of Dart.
[2] cf. Shakespeare, *The Merchant of Venice*, Act I, Scene I.

Plate 39   **MICHAELSTOW**
Jane Merifeld 1662

Lewis Dart was the son of John Wallis, alias Dart, of Barnstaple and his wife Joan Courtney. His father bequeathed to him one thousand five hundred pounds and all his best apparel when he " accomplished the age of 21 years."[3] Lewis married Elizabeth, the eldest daughter of Thomas Roscarrock of Roscarrock. Of their six sons, only five are named: John, Charles, Phillip, Lewis and Francis; and one daughter Jane. Elizabeth survived her husband by fourteen years. Francis, the youngest son died in 1605 at the age of six. Jane Dart married John Tremayne of Heligan.[4]

In his will dated 30th September 1631,[5] Lewis named only two of his children, bequeathing one house in Barnstaple to Phillip and the sum of twenty pounds to Jane; his wife he appointed sole executrix. Charles[6] married and had one daughter Ann, who died unmarried in 1681 when the estate passed to the Tremayne family.

In his survey of 1602, Richard Carew writes: " Of Pentuan I have spoken before. For the present, it harboureth Master Dart, who as divers Gentlemen, well descended, and accomodated in Devon, doe yet rather make choyce of a pleasing and retired equalitie in the little Cornish Angle."[7]

The old manor house was burnt down during the early part of the eighteenth century. Although it may not have been comparable in size with some other Cornish dwellings of that time, it was a house of no mean accommodation. This is evident from the inventory taken at the time of Lewis Dart's death, in which a gallery and chapel chamber are listed among more than two dozen rooms.

MICHAELSTOW
Jane Merifeld 1662
(Plate 39)

Arms: Argent, a chevron Sable between 3 Cornish choughs proper.
Position: Set against the west wall of the north aisle.
Size: 5 feet by 2 feet 10 inches.
Condition: Fair.
Style: Inside a border inscription with elaborated capitals are two incised female figures. In spite of the extremely crude drawing, the smaller figure is certainly that of a child.[1]
Inscription: Here lyeth Jane ye daughter of John Killiow esqr. &
late wife to Thomas Merifeld of Collomb maior gent. who died
ye 26th of March 1662.

[3] C.R.O. wills.
[4] C.R.O. Tremayne Papers.
[5] C.R.O. wills.
[6] Capt. of Foot in Royalist Army.
[7] Carew, p. 140.
[1] This could represent Jane Merifeld as a child, perhaps commemorating her recovery from a serious illness (as on the Mary Arundell slate at Duloe) or it may represent a daughter who could have erected the monument.

H

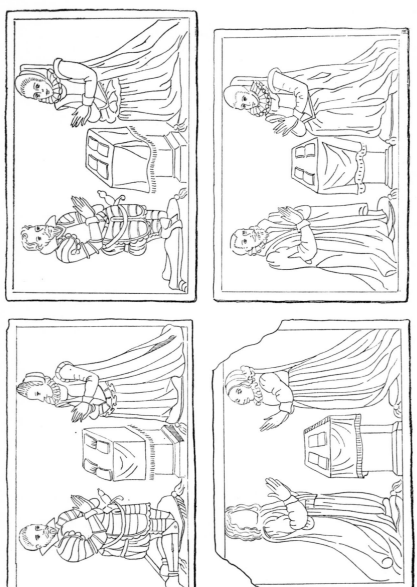

MINSTER

Four slate tablets from the tomb of John Hender 1611

Plate 40

MINSTER

John Hender 1611

(Plate 40)

Arms: Azure, a lion rampant within an orle of escallops Or.

Position: At the east end of the south aisle.

Condition: Very good.

Style: Carved in stone beneath an arch supported by pilasters are the figures of John Hender and his wife, kneeling at a prayer desk. Above is a shield of arms and below a slate panel bearing the inscription in block letters. On each of the pilasters are fixed two tablets of slate bearing the incised figures of John Hender's daughters and their husbands. There was originally a shield of arms over each couple and also above the main figures. The carving on the small slates is of expert craftsmanship, closely resembling the style of monumental brasses. Three of the tablets are in excellent condition; on the other, the carving is no longer very clear.

The figures of the eldest daughter Katherine and her husband, John Molesworth, are cut on the first tablet, fixed at the top left-hand side of the monument and measuring 6 inches by 3¾ inches. They face each other kneeling at a prayer desk upon which lie two open books. The woman wears a farthingale and loose cloak with a ruff and her hair combed high under a Tudor-style bonnet. The man wears a beard, high stiff collar and a suit of armour.

The second daughter, Frances, with her husband Richard Robartes, is shown on the tablet at the top right-hand side which measures 6¼ inches by 3¾ inches. She wears a ruff and farthingale and a Tudor head-dress and faces her husband across a prayer desk. The man is shown with curling hair and a beard and wearing armour.

The third daughter Mary, and her husband Elice Hele, are carved on the slate fixed at the bottom left-hand side which measure 5¾ inches by 4 inches. Both kneel at a prayer desk the woman wearing a small ruff with her simple loosely fitting gown and a soft draping over her long hair. The man is dressed in a long fully-cut robe and wears his hair long.

The fourth daughter Elizabeth, and her husband William Cotton, are drawn on the slate at the bottom right-hand side which measures 6 inches by 4 inches. The woman kneels at a prayer desk wearing a ruff, farthingale and loose cloak and high-styled hair with traditional bonnet.

The man wears a beard, with his hair closely cut, and is dressed in a flowing robe with a ruff and skull cap.

Inscription: Here under lieth enterred the body of John Hender Esq late Lord and Owner of the Honour and ffee of Botreaux Castle and Worthevale in this County a Justice of Peace and Quorum whilst he lived there and Patron of this church, who deceased ye 7th day of June 1611. He was trulie religious and of great integrite & whilst he lived imployed as a principall agent in all weightie affaires of state, in this his countrie. He had issue by Jane his deerest consort, (ye daughter of Thom. Thorne late of Yardle in ye county of Northampton Esq.) 4 daughters his heirs Katherine ye eldest married unto John Molesworth Esq. His Maties Surveiour Generall of this county. Francis ye second espoused unto Richard Robartes Esq. now High Shrief ther. Mary ye third coupled unto Elice Hele Esqr. learned in ye lawes & Trear of ye Temple, London. & Elizabeth ye fourth affianced in marriage unto Mr. Willm Cotton sone and heire to ye right Reverend Father in God William Lord Bishooppe of Exon.

Hender, whose body sometyme did inshrine
the vertues, truly morall and devine,
hath heer a place of rest: his honor'd name
is by those vertues now bequeathed to fame:
and ev'rie good man that by chance is sent
to see this grave, becomes his monument.

John Hender was the eldest son and heir of William Hender of Bottreaux Castle, and his wife, Agnes, daughter of John Newcourt of Holsworthy.[1] Richard Carew in his Survey of Cornwall 1602 refers to " . . . my kind friend, Master John Hender, a gentleman for his good parts employed by her Majesty amongst others in the peace government of the shire."

Katherine, the eldest daughter, and wife of John Molesworth Esq. of Pencarrow, had two sons and two daughters. She predeceased her father and her eldest son Hender became co-heir of his grandfather.

Frances the second daughter, and wife of Richard Roberts Esq. afterwards Baron Robartes of Truro, had two sons and three daughters.

Mary the third daughter, was the first wife of Eliceaus (Elice) Hele Esq. of Fardel near Plymouth; lawyer and Justice of the Peace for Devon.[2] Their children died young.

Elizabeth, the fourth daughter and wife of William Cotton, Precentor of Exeter Cathedral, had three sons and five daughters.

In his will,[3] John Hender directed that four poor people, born in the parish and nominated by his executor, should each receive the sum of eightpence weekly for ever, to be paid to them every Sabbath day in the Church of Minster at the end of Morning Prayer. He further directed

[1] *Visitations C.*, p. 217.
[2] Prince, *Worthies of Devon*, 1810, p. 487.
[3] C.R.O. wills.

" . . . that two of them be seafaring men or their widdowes (if it may be) and the other two of the land . . . also my will is that the fower poore people aforesaid for the tyme beinge shall have for ever ffower rooms parcel of the wch I have lately built for an Almshouse together with certain plotts of land for gardens."

This charity was to be maintained by his youngest daughter Elizabeth, and her husband William Cotton. It was afterwards known as the Cotton Charity and in 1701 accommodated six poor persons; three receiving one shilling, and three eightpence weekly. By the year 1900 the Almshouses had fallen into ruins and in 1931 the site was sold and the money invested for the continuance of the Charity.

The mansion house called Bottreaux Castle was situate on the west side of the High Street or hill leading through the town. The site was cut through in making the new road. On the opposite side of the street were the stables and gardens in which there continues a gigantic pear tree.[4]

William and Elizabeth Cotton 1656

Arms: Argent, a bend Sable between 3 ogresses.

Against the South wall is a larger monument of similar design, to the memory of William Cotton and his wife Elizabeth who died 1656.

The figure of the man, wearing cap and gown, is a replica in stone of the slate carving on the Hender memorial. Below the Latin inscription is a touching epitaph cut on a slate panel, and a family of eight children, carved in stone, and a row of small shields. Below the three sons' shields is written " 3 Diatrite " and under the daughters' " 5 Diapente " with " 8 Diapason " and $\dfrac{3}{8}$[5]

In Perfect concord may they still agree
Whose very numbers teach them harmony.
                    Epitaph:
Forty-nine yeares they lived man and wife,
And what's more rare thus many without strife:
She first departing, hee a few weeks tryed
To live without her—could not—and so dyed.
Both in their wedlocks great sabatick rest,
To be where theres no wedlock ever blest;
And having here a jubily begun,
Theyr taken hence that it may nere be don.

---

[4] Maclean, Vol. I, pt. II.
[5] The harmonic triad—the common chord of harmony 8.5.3.

St. Minver

Figured panel from the tomb of Elizabeth and Thomas Stone 1604

Plate 41

ST. MINVER

Elizabeth and Thomas Stone 1586 1604

(Plate 41)

Arms: Party per pale Or and Vert, a chevron engrailed between 3 birds countercharged, quartering Sable fess between 3 bears Or.

Position: Set low against the wall at the east end of the north aisle.

Size: 5 feet 3 inches by 3 feet 7 inches.

Condition: Badly damaged.

Style: Originally the front panel of a tomb-chest. Cut in bold relief, inside a wide border of strapwork, are the kneeling figures of Thomas Stone and his wife, Elizabeth. The man kneels on a cushion before the remaining fragments of a prayer stool, with a book on it. Above it is a shield charged with the arms of Stone. The whole of the upper part of the man's body and his leg has flaked off. The woman wears the traditional head-dress of the period, a ruff, and a gown with elaborate epaulettes and a chain with an ornamented cross attached.

Between the two figures is a second shield, bearing the arms of Stone impaling Harris, and behind the woman a third shield, charged with the arms of Harris. Beside this slate panel are two other smaller pieces belonging to the same tomb and set in the wall, one above the other. On the top piece is carved the family crest: " On a rock ppr. a salmon, holding in his mouth a rose " and a shield quartering the arms of Stone with Whitlinge and Harris. This stone was apparently part of the original backplate. The lower piece bears the shield of Stone and was one of the end panels.

The upper slab of the tomb was found in a building near the Church among a quantity of rough paving stones and other lumber, broken and greatly damaged. It was circumscribed: " Here lyeth ye body of Thomas Stone, Gentleman, who died XXVIII of Julie 1604 and Elizabetha his wife, died the XVI day—86 " and upon an ornamental shield, within the border, the arms of Stone and Harris impaled. He was buried 28th July 1604 and she 16th January 1586.[1]

Thomas Stone of Trevigoe was the only son of John and great-grandson of Roger Stone and his wife Joan Whitlinge. He married Elizabeth, daughter of William Harris of Hayne, and by her had two sons and two daughters. John, the second son, died abroad and William inherited Trevigoe which he held until 1625 or a little later, when the lease apparently expired. The estate was held by the family of Stone as early as 1473 and was formerly a customary tenement of the manor of Blisland.[2] Norden records " Travegie the house wherein Stone in-habiteth, but the Lande is Sr Michaell Stanhops."

[1] Maclean, Vol. III, p. 26.
[2] Maclean, Vol. III, p.275.

Trevigoe lies 1¼ miles south from the church in a sheltered position, below the road to Portquin. There seems nothing remaining of the old house in the present-day farm buildings.

John Silly 1672

Arms: Azure, a chevron between 3 mullets Or.

Position: High up on the wall of the south aisle.

Size: 5 feet 6 inches by 2 feet 9 inches.

Condition: Good. Black slate.

Style: At the top of the tablet, between two urns of foliage, is a shield with crest, displaying the arms of Silly impaling Cotton. Underneath, the Latin inscription and epitaph is set in an oval, between two charming borders of the trailing vine pattern and surmounted by an angel's head.

Inscription: P.M.
Johannis Silly de Trevelver Ex hoc agro Cornub parochiaq S.Minver Armigeri. Qui Ex uxore sua Jana filia Gulielmi Cotton Cantoris ecclesiae Cathedralis Sci Petri Exon. Octo suscepit et sex reliquit Liberos, Filios tres, nempe, Gulielmum, Joh'em et Marcum Totidemq; natas Elizabetham, Janam et Catharinam; Dum in hominum Coetu Compostione Intervicinos litium Egregia humilitate et charitate clarus per Quinquaginta Annos Floruit; obiitque undecimo die Aprilis Anno D'ni 1672. Uxor ejus relicta flebilis (Pietatis ergo) hoc posuit monumentum.[3]

The work is signed William Vague Sculpt.

John Silly of Trevelver, the son of John, married Jane daughter of the Rev. William Cotton, Precentor of Exeter Cathedral,[4] and had three sons, William, Toby and Marck; and three daughters, Elizabeth, Jane and Catherine. He died in 1672.

Trevelver lies about a mile and a half south from the church overlooking the Heyle or estuary. Only a small part of the old mansion house remains, and that considerably altered and converted into a farm house.

[3] Maclean, Vol. III, p. 29.
[4] Monument in Minster Church.

MORVAL

Walter Coode 1637

(Plate 42)

Arms: Argent, a chevron Gules between 3 cocks Sable armed crested and jelloped of the second; quartering, Gules 3 crescents Or.

Position: Fixed high up on the west wall of the transept.

Size: 6 feet by 2 feet 6 inches.

Condition: Good, except for large crack across the middle. Traces of colour remain.

Style: Inside a border inscription are the very simply carved figures of Walter Coode and his wife Phillippa, kneeling one on either side of a prayer desk, with two open books upon it. The man wears the Stuart style of dress, with a sword, and his hair long. The woman wears her widow's wimple over a perfectly plain gown. Above them is an achievement of arms showing Coode impaling Vivian. In the left-hand corner is a shield with the arms of Coode, and in the opposite corner a lozenge[1] with the arms of Vivian. Behind the man is a stem of trailing vine bearing six fruits (four with skulls above them) representing his deceased sons; and a similar stem, representing four daughters, is behind the woman. Above the children are eight lines of an epitaph in Latin.

The four corners of the border inscription are filled with two shields and two lozenges, displaying the arms of Coode and Vivian.

Inscription: Heere lyeth the body of Walltr Coode sone & heire to William Coode of morvall esquire was buried ye 27th of august in ye yeare of our lord Ano: 1637
Anobis genita haec non baptizala suere Technia; seit solus quam numerola Deus. Sors cadem cunctis: una omnes uexat Erynnis Infantes pariter Mors junenesq rapit.

Walter Coode was the eldest son of William Coode, and his wife Loveday Kendall of Pelyn. He married Phillippa, a daughter of Hannibal Vivian[2] and by her had eight children, none of whom survived. He died in 1637 at the age of 43.

Morval House, which is a well preserved example of a Tudor house, although with subsequent alterations, is set in a delightful valley and close by the church.

---

[1] Denoting a widow.
[2] *Visitations C.,* p. 95.

MORVAL
Walter Coode 1637

Plate 42

MORWENSTOW

John Kempthorne 1591

(Plate 43)

Arms: Argent, a chevron between 3 bears' heads bendways couped Sable, muzzled Or and Argent, 3 pine trees proper.

Position: Fixed to the wall behind the altar in the north aisle.

Condition: Rather worn.

Style: The top end of a ledger stone, and within the remains of a border inscription incised, the upper half of a bearded man wearing a ruff and loose gown. Behind his head are the letters I.K. A.L.LEY and above them two shields of arms. The left hand shield shows the arms of Kempthorne, with a crescent for difference; and the shield on the right, the arms of Kempthorne impaling Ley and Courtney quarterly. Of the border inscription only the name and date remain.

John Kempthorne of Tonacombe was the eldest son of John Ley alias Kempthorne, of Kempthorne in Devon. This family was originally of Legh in Bere Ferrers, but a younger branch settled at Kempthorne and was afterwards known by that name.

John married Katharine, daughter of Sir Piers Courtney of Chudleigh in Devon, but died without issue. His brother Thomas was vicar of Morwenstow.[1]

" The Barton of Tonacombe correctly pronounced Tunnacombe is now, though without warrant—styled a manor. The name is probably derived from the Saxon Tun-a-combe, the Town or Settlement of the Valley . . . The Combe or Valley is some little way from the present house. Tonacombe is now all one large farm but so early as 1296 the 3 vills of Tunnacombis are named . . . At a later date, 1620, we find no less than 6 separate tenements of Tonacombe. Of these 5 then belonged to the Leys or Kempthornes . . . The oldest part of Tonacombe House (viz. the wing on the south side) seems to be of this date (Hen. VII or Hen. VIII) and possibly also the Great Hall. John Ley married Katharine daughter of Sir Piers Courtney and their arms adorn the fine panelling of the Parlour. Katharine's mother, Lady Courtney, lived at Tonacombe and her arms may be seen on the panelling of the east bedroom."[2]

[1] *Visitations C.*, p. 288.
[2] Henderson, E. Cornwall, Vol., p. 405.

Plate 43   MORWENSTOW
                    John Kempthorne 1591

ST. NEOT

William Bere 1610

(Plate 44)

Arms: Argent, a bear saliant Sable, a crescent for difference.

Position: At the west end of the nave, formerly in the east near the altar.

Size: 6 feet 6 inches by 6 feet 5 inches.

Condition: Excellent. Black slate from the local quarry.

Style: A tomb-chest complete with backplate, enclosed in a protective frame of wood. Carved on the backplate, in bold relief, are the figures of William Bere and his wife, set within a frame-work of traditional scroll design.

The man, wearing a ruff, doublet and knee breeches, kneels before a prayer stool on which is a closed book. His wife kneels behind him wearing a head-dress, ruff and full-skirted gown. Behind the figures are three shields; the one on the left is blank; the centre one shows the arms of Bere impaled and the third shield the arms of Bere. Carved on the front panel are the figures of their three children:—Thomas, kneeling before a prayer stool with book, and a skull above it, wears a doublet and trunk-hose. Behind him kneel Grace and Phillippa, each wearing a full-skirted gown with high collar and jewellery. Behind them are three shields, the one next to Phillippa showing Bellot impaling Bere; the centre shield, Grylls impaling Bere and the third, the arms of Bere.

Inscription: Hic jacet corpus Willelmi Bere generosi, mortui in domino anno domini milesimo sexcentesimo decimo die Octobris vigessimo quarto: sum quod eris.

> Here lyeth Bere whom Angelles to heaven beare,
> Banisht though earth, yet now made heaven's heire;
> Faithfull he was to frends, skilfull in lawe of man;
> Practis'd in law of god, & so heavens heritag wonn.
> Hence learne of the dead good deeds to imitate,
> Hence learne of the dead gaynst death this caveat,
> Nothing more certayn then is death to all;
> No more uncertayn then death's hower of call.
> Now whilst thou liv'st then learn to dye to sinne,
> With Christ, through Christ, in grace to live beginn
> Soe when thou diest thy death no death shall be,
> But passage unto life, the god of lyfe to see.

William Bere Esq. of Lawharne, was the son of John Bere of Pengelly in St. Neot, and Elizabeth, daughter of John Arundell of Helland. There is no evidence of the name of William's wife, by whom he had one son Thomas and two daughters; Grace, who married Sir John

Plate 44   ST. NEOT
Figured panels from the tomb of William Bere 1610

Grylls of Lanreath; and Phillippa who married Renatus Bellot of Bochym in Cury. Thomas died without issue.[1]

In addition to his estate of Lawahren or Lawharne, William Bere owned the manor of Faweton or Trenay, to which was annexed the advowson of the church.

NORTHILL

Jane and Thomas Vincent 1601 1606

(Plate 45)

Arms: Azure, 3 quarterfoils Argent 2 and 1.

Position: At the west end of the north aisle.

Size: 10 feet by 6 feet.

Condition: Excellent.

Style: A tomb-chest with backplate. This monument is elaborately carved in low relief and has a tapered backplate of unusual design. The top portion bears 4 Biblical references in Latin and an allegorical carving of Christ overcoming sin and death, in the form of a dragon and a skeleton exposed in a coffin. The whole design is surrounded by a trailing vine decoration. Carved on the lower part are the figures of Thomas Vincent, his wife Jane and their fifteen children, all set within a border of elaborate strapwork. The man kneels on a cushion before a prayer stool and wears a ruff with his doublet and trunk-hose; his hair is worn long and he has a beard. Behind him kneel eight sons in similar dress, and above the fifth son is set a skull.

Facing the man across a second prayer stool, the woman kneels on a cushion, with seven daughters kneeling behind her, all wearing ruffs, Tudor bonnets and full-skirted gowns. Over the first daughter is a skull. Above the husband and wife is carved the figure of death, holding in its left hand a scythe and a serpent, and in its right hand a dart pointing towards the husband.

The top panel of the tomb bears a border inscription, and within it a centre panel of strapwork between some lines of Latin verse. At the right-hand end are the decorated capitals TV and on the opposite side an angel's head. The four corners of the border are filled with designs of fleur-de-lis, rose, vine, and a two-leaved acorn.

On the front panel three shields are displayed, separated by carved pilasters and showing the arms of Lampen, Vincent, and Lower.

Two quaint and unusual heads, male and female, are carved above the pilasters.

The end panel shows an oak tree in fruit with five acorns lying at its base, and above it two more curious heads, male and female.

This tomb is recorded by Edmund Spoure in 1694[2] as being in the chancel, and a drawing of it shows the skeleton of death, as a detached

---

[1] *Visitations C.*, p. 29.
[2] Edmund Spoure, *The Trebartha Book*, MS.

Plate 45   NORTHILL
Jane and Thomas Vincent 1606

symbol, set up on the edge of the back-plate and another figure standing on the opposite end, carrying an hour-glass and a flail.

Inscription: Here lye the bodies of Thomas Vyncent, Gentleman, and Jane his Wife, by whom he had Issue 8 Sons & 7 Daughters. He departed this life ye 29th of March 1606. She ye 7th of Januarie, 1601.

> Confidete vici mundu: Jo.16
> Obi tua more victoria: 1 Cor.15
> Côteret caput tuum: Gen. 3.
> Ero morsus Infern tuus: Ose. 13.
> Lugeat ista legens qui sunt lugenda legenda
> Lectaq: lectori causa doloris erunt.
> Prospera per charo recubant cum conguge consors
> Atque prior moritur mortuus alter erat.
> Amplexere simul viventes et morientes
> Vixerunt domino ac occubuere deo.
> Cur mortem auctuis mortalis;
> Mors meditanda est;
> Non metuenda tibi;
> Sed metuenda malo.
> Heres defuncti perculsus amore parentum
> Hoc opus exiguum sic cumulavit humo.

Thomas Vincent was the son of John Vincent, of Stoke Dabernon in Surrey, a barrister who travelled the Western Circuit and married the heiress of Battens in Northill.[3] He married Jane, the eldest daughter of John Lampen and his wife Jane Lower. They had 8 sons, Thomas, John, Nathaniell, Henry, Methusalem, Richard, William and George: and 7 daughters:—Katheryne, Lydia, Frances, Mary, Deberra and Jane. The first-born daughter died young as shown by a skull above her figure on the slate. The fifth son Methusalem, unlike his namesake, also died young.

In his will made in 1603[4] Thomas laments ". . . not long since in that it pleased Almighty God (to my greate discomforte) to call unto Himselfe . . . my deare and lovinge wife, with whome I lyved many yeares in peace and love, and had (god be thanked) plentifull fruite of the married life, besides many other blessinges of wealth and livinge."

He gave to each of his two eldest daughters one hundred and fifty pounds, and to the other eleven younger children, one hundred pounds each. To his eldest son, and sole executor, Thomas, he bequeathed all his lands rents and services; ". . . whome I require uppon my blessinge to use his brothers and sisters kindely and courteously and to be instead of a father unto them after I am gone . . ."

In addition to his family legacies, Thomas Vincent founded a charity for the relief of the poor of Northill.

[3] Collectanea, p. 1150.
[4] P.C.C.

The will ends, "... And as touchinge my debts due unto me uppon my severall bookes of Accomptes since my practys in Attornishippe, beinge manye, and yet not greate some of them old, some of the debtors dead and some poore not able to paie. I wishe and require therefor myne Executor not to Demand or challenge any more of my said Debts uppon my bookes of Accompts for Lawe causes, than he shall finde in a little paper booke which I purpose God willinge to write with my owne hand. ... And the residue of my said debts for law causes uppon my bookes of Accompt beinge many in number I freely forgive unto everie one of them owinge the same."

Battens lies within half a mile east of the church and close to the road. A drawing made in 1694 shows a low-built L-shaped house with projecting porch. Some traces of this old house remain in the present-day farm, notably the granite doorway inscribed:—

ANO:D:1581   T. VYNCENT

Richard Spoure 1623

Arms: Gules, on a chevron Or a rose of the first, between two mullets pierced Sable.

Position: Attached to the east wall of the south, or Trebartha, aisle.

Size: 5 feet 2 inches by 2 feet 7 inches.

Condition: Very good.

Style: Carved in relief, the border is of a simple interlaced strap and leaf design, coloured ivory, blue and red. Inset are four ivory-coloured pilasters supporting three patterned arches. Between the arches are carved two quaint angels' heads highly coloured, with yellow and red wings. On a panel below the centre arch are the arms and crest of Spoure quartering Speccot, in full colour. The panel on the left bears the inscription in a decorative style and that on the right, a rhyming epitaph poorly lettered.

Inscription: Heere lieth ye body of Richard Spoure, ye son and
heire of Hen-ry Spoure, Esq and Elizabeth; who was buried ye
20th day of Aprill, in Anno Domini 1623; et Aetatis suae 3d
moneth. Infans quid loquitur

This carved tombe The sad inscription bears,
Of my soone death, And of my Parents' tears.
For my departure, Though that happy I
By that was freed From future misery:
And now instead of their Fond Dandling kisses,
I now enjoy a heaven,—A heaven of blisses.
Waile not therefore for me, But heavens implore,
That God with other issue You would store:
Whose pious lives may cause You joyful eyes
And tend your deaths With sacred obsequies.

Richard was the infant son of Henry Spoure of Trebartha and his wife Elizabeth Speccot. Of their family of three sons and five daughters only one child, the youngest son Edmund, reached maturity.[5]

Against the south wall of the Trebartha aisle is a large slate panel commemorating Henry Spoure (great-greatgrandfather of the infant Richard) who died 1603. He built the Great Parlour at Trebartha and amassed a considerable fortune from the success of his Lemarne Tin Mine.[6]

Trebartha lies a mile north-west of the church, by the river Lynher. The old mansion was taken down during the eighteenth century and another built on the site by Francis Rodd, who inherited the estate from his cousin Mrs. Mary Grylls, the only surviving child of Edmund Spoure. The second house was demolished after the Second World War.

(*Plate 46*)

Position: Fixed against the east wall of the Trebartha aisle.

Size: A fragment of slate measuring 2 feet 3 inches by 1 foot 5 inches.

Style: Incised upon it are traces of lettering and a small shrouded figure. There seems little doubt that it represents a child wrapped in its chrisom.[7]

Edmund Spoure, writing in 1694, describes the slate thus: " This is a very ancient Tombe as appeares by the Charrecter which I doubt will be very difficult for any one to interprett, it was found amongst old rubbish, not farre from my Chapple at Trebartha, as T.B. perhaps may goe for Trebartha, it is now but part of a Tombe, the Shape and forme of which you see here underneath drawne."

[5] *Visitations C.*, p. 431.
[6] Edmund Spoure, *The Trebartha Book*, MS.
[7] See page 5.

Plate 47   NORTH PETHERWIN
Dorothy Killigrew 1634

NORTH PETHERWIN
Dorothy Killigrew 1634
(Plate 47)

Arms: Argent, an eagle displayed with 2 heads Sable a bordure of the second bezantee.

Position: Fixed to the east wall of the south aisle, behind the organ.

Size: 7 feet by 3 feet 3 inches.

Condition: Very worn.

Style: Inside a border inscription are some immature lines of rather florid verse, and two female figures[1] cut in low relief. The larger figure is shown full-length and the smaller one kneeling; both are very crudely drawn and all the details of face and dress are worn away. Beside the figures is a shield displaying the arms of Killigrew quartered with Monck.

Inscription: Here lyeth buried ye body of Dorothy the wife of John
Killigrew of Arwennick Esq. who ended her mortall life on the
second day of Aprill Anno Domini 1634
> Monck's daughter Killigrews unspotted bride
> & Poycfields heire deaths one stroke did divide
> From frayle mortality to be enthroned
> Under this burthen but now lowdly sing
> halleliuahs to heavens King
> Odelia placed this here who lives to plaine
> Her mothers losse with whom she longs to raigne.

Dorothy was the daughter and heir of Sir Thomas Monck of Potheridge in Devon. Her marriage to John Killigrew of Arweneck, (who died in 1605) is described by Martin Killigrew writing in 1737: " John, ye eldest Son of ye said Sir John Killigrew marryed Dorothy, daughter of Thomas Monck of Poderidge in ye County of Devon Esq. Ancestor to Gen Monck, Duke of Albermarle, by whom he had 9 sons and 5 daughters; who tho' a father of so many Children, was so negligent of his Affairs, a fine Gentleman, a Gamester, and so profuse in his Way of living as to leave his eldest son ye last Sir John Killigrew of ye name, a very shattered Estate. . . ."[2]

One of the daughters of this marriage, Elizabeth, married Edmund Yeo of North Petherwin.

Richard Carew, writing in 1602 said, "—Arwenacke entertaineth you with a pleasing view; for the same standeth so far within the haven's mouth, that it is protected from the sea storms, and yet so near thereunto, as it yieldeth a ready passage out. . . . It is owned by Master John Killigrew who married the daughter of Monck, and heir to her mother." Part of the old house, which overlooks Falmouth harbour, still stands but it is now divided into flats.

---

[1] As at Duloe & Michaelstow.
[2] J.R.I.C. No. XII, p. 272.

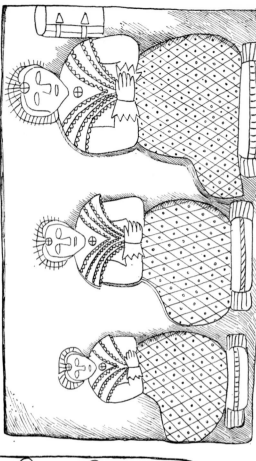

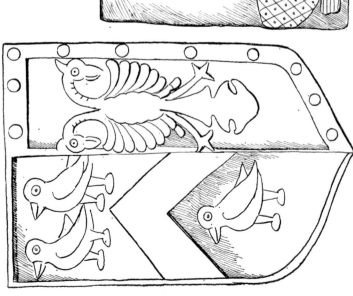

NORTH PETHERWIN
Ann, Susanna and Margaret Yeo 1638

Plate 48

Ann, Susanna and Margaret Yeo 1633 1634 1638

(Plate 48)

Arms: Argent, a chevron between 3 shovellers Sable.

Position: In the north transept, now used as a vestry.

Size: 5 feet 10 inches by 3 feet.

Condition: Good. Apparently whitewashed at some period.

Style: Below the inscription is an angel's head, a shield bearing the arms of Yeo impaling Killigrew, and three female figures. Very coarsely carved in low relief, the girls wear simple caps and full-skirted gowns and kneel side by side on large cushions; beside the eldest girl is a closed book.

Inscription: Here lyeth ye body of An Yeo who was buried on ye 26 day of June An domi 1633 being of ye age of 14 years. Here lyeth also ye body of Susanna Yeo who was buried on the 10 day of January ano domi 1634 being of the age of 20 years. Here lyeth also ye body of Margaret Yeo who was buried on ye 19th day of May ano domi 1638 being age of 22 years. All which were ye daughters of Edmund Yeo of this pish Esq. and Elizabeth his wife.

> Susan. Margaret. An.
> Here ly entombed three sisters all sweet girles
> For graces rare for goodness matchles perles
> The youngest first did make up her account
> And did ascend God's sion holy mount
> The eldest next not willing here to stay
> Went on with cheere yt hard but happy way
> The second last on cherub wings did fly
> Unto the place of joy the starie skie
> Theire soules are mett theire bodies sleepe in dust
> And shall not wake till rise again the just
> When in ye aire they shall theire Jesus see
> And with a com ye blessed blessed be.

Ann, Susanna and Margaret were three of the eight daughters of Edmund, son of Leonard Yeo, and his wife Elizabeth Killigrew, of the Barton of North Petherwin. This family was a younger branch of the Yeos of Hatherleigh.[3] Their maternal grandmother was Dorothy, the wife of John Killigrew, whose monument is in the South aisle.

---

[3] *Visitations D.*, p. 837.

Plate 49

PELYNT
Francis Buller 1616

PELYNT

Francis Buller 1616

(Plate 49)

Arms: Sable, on a cross Argent pierced of the field, four eagles displayed of the first.

Position: Against the north wall of the chancel, inside the altar rail,

Size: 12 feet by 6 feet.

Condition: Good. Coloured.

Style: Carved in bold relief, the tomb-chest is surmounted by an elaborate backplate divided into four panels. At the top is a shield of arms quartering Buller and flanked by rather grotesque male and female figures. The next panel shows four small shields impaling Buller. Six similar shields are set, three on each side of the two figures, on the next and largest panel.

Francis Buller is shown kneeling before a prayer desk, bearded and wearing a sword, ruff, black doublet and knee breeches. His wife, Thomasine, kneels behind him in a black brocaded gown, wearing the traditional head-dress and gold ornaments. Below are carved the small figures of eight daughters and four sons, between bands of strapwork decoration. The faces of these children are of plaster.

On the top of the chest is cut an epitaph in the form of an acrostic, with a pattern of flowers on either side and bordered by the inscription. Another ten shields are shown on the west end and the front of the chest. On a third panel, stapled to the east wall, are six other shields. Beneath each of the sixteen shields is written the marriage alliance. At some period the floor of the chancel has been raised ten inches, cutting off the border of strapwork along the bottom of the tomb. The slate is in good condition although some damage shows near the man's figure, and the colouring has become rather shabby since it was renovated 150 years ago.

Inscription: 1616

Here lyeth the Body of Fraunces Buller of Tregarrick, Esquier, who departed this lyfe the twenty-seaventh septem. in the fayth of God our Saviour, one thousand sixe hundred and fifteenth.

F—lie not from death that brings thee blisse;
r —egard not life that death procures;
a —mend that life that lives amisse;
n—o joy to life that life assures;
c —ease to imbrace these wretched dayes;
i —n peace and love increase them still;
s —eale up thy god in soule always,
B—efore on thee he worke his will.
u—ntill god call thee from this place,
l —et vertues steps direct thy life;
l —ive still in love which may purchase
e —ternall bliss with Christ above.
r —emember this and all is well.

Francis Buller of Tregarrick was the second son of Richard Buller, and his wife Margaret Trethurffe. He married Thomasine, daughter of Thomas Williams of Devon, and had four sons and eight daughters. He was High Sheriff in 1600. In his will dated 1615[1] Francis Buller directed that his body should be buried ". . . in the Church of Pelint or in the Chauncell there before my seate." Sir Richard Buller of Shillingham, eldest son and heire, was M.P. for Saltash 1625—1627 and Fowey 1640 until his death in 1642. During the Civil War, he was a general of the Parliamentarian army. He married Alice Haward of London and had seven sons and six daughters.

Mathew, second son of Francis, married—and had one son. Francis, who inherited Tregarrick, was a leading Parliamentarian. He married Sibill, daughter of John Nicholls of St. Kew and had five sons and two daughters.

The fourth son is not named.

Margaret the eldest daughter married Richard Kendall of Treworgie and secondly Sir Thomas Honeywood of Kent. She had a daughter named Thomasine.

Thomasine Buller married Robert Dodson of Hay in St. Ive; she had two sons and three daughters.

Mary married Arthur Burrell of St. Stephen-by-Saltash and had six sons and four daughters.

Margery married Piers Manington of Combeshead and had two sons and two daughters.

Frances married John Vyvyan of St. Columb and had one daughter.

Emlyn married Henry Chiverton of Quethiock and had two sons. The two other daughters of Francis are not named.[2]

Tregarrick, now a modern farm, is about a mile west from the church. Richard Carew described its situation thus: " The warmth of this hundred, siding the south, hath enticed many gentlemen here to make choice of their dwellings, as Mr. Buller, now sheriff, at Tregarrick."[3]

[1] P.C.C.
[2] *Visitations C.*, p. 57.
[3] Carew, p. 131.

William Achym 1589
(Plate 50)

Arms: Argent, a maunch between 9 cinquefoils 3, 3 and 3 Gules.

Position: Attached to the south wall of the chancel and formerly in the Achym aisle, now the vestry.

Size: 5 feet 6 inches by 2 feet 6 inches.

Condition: Excellent.

Style: Part of a dismantled tomb-chest. Inside a narrow border with a Latin inscription is cut the full-length figure of a bearded man in armour. With the helmet laid like a pillow behind his head, and the long sword and misericord, or mercy dagger, this slate has a mediaeval style about it.[4]

Two small shields display the arms of Achym quartered, and Achym impaling Bligh. Above the slate is another panel with a large shield of the same arms and the crest, a lion sejant, in colour.

Inscription: hic iacet Gulleelmus Achim, Armiger, qui obiit die mensis decimo septimo Novembris, Anno Domini, Millessimo Quingentessimo Octogessimo nono; Aetatis suae 63.

William was a son of William Achym of Bodmin, who acquired considerable land in Pelynt at the time of the Dissolution of the Monasteries.[5] He married Emline a daughter of John Bligh of Bodmin and by her had four sons and three daughters.[6] In his will dated 1586,[7] three years before his death at the age of 63, he is described as " William the Elder," having a brother then living of the same name. He bequeathed his lands in Egloshayle, Bodmin and St. Giles-in-the-Heath to his wife " —makinge no waste nor spoile in cuttinge downe tymber trees or otherwise." His estate of Muchlarnick in Pelynt he gave to his second son William. Thomas, his heir, inherited the family home at Hall to which was annexed the advowson of the church. Hall is within sight of the church, to the east.

Edward Trelawny 1630

Arms: Argent, a chevron Sable between 3 oakleaves proper.

Position: Against the south wall of the chancel inside the altar rail.

Size: 4 feet by 3 feet.

Condition: Very good.

Style: This monument of slate and plaster-work consists of a beautifully incised inscription on a slate tablet with a small ornamental border of acorns, fruit and flowers. Above is a shield with the crest and arms of Trelawny impaling Arscott and the date " june the 7th 1630 "

---

[4] See also Bevill tomb at Talland.
[5] Geoffrey Grigson, *Freedom of the Parish*, p. 48.
[6] *Visitations C.*, p. 1.
[7] P.C.C.

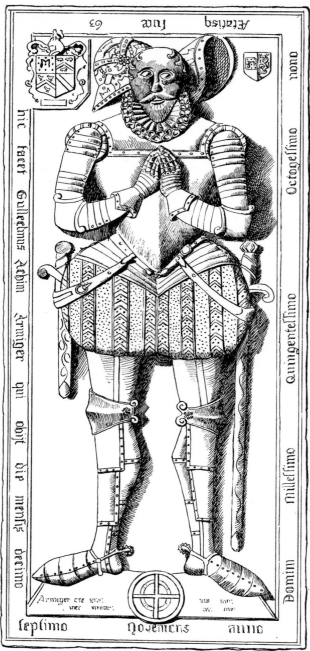

Plate 50   **PELYNT**
William Achym 1589

surrounded by elaborate ornamentation, carved in relief. The whole
design is set in a boldly carved frame of plaster and is in splendid
condition, retaining most of its colouring of red, gold, green and blue.
The lettering is delightful and one of the best examples to be found
among the slate memorials.

Inscription: iunne the 7. 1630
    Edward Trelawnye
    Ana: We wander, Alter, Dy.
        O what a bubble, vapour, puffe of breath,
        a nest of wormes, a lumpe of pallid earth
        is mud: wald man: before wee mount on high
        we cope with change, We wander, Alter, Dy.
        Causidicum claudit tumulus (miraris?) honestum
        gentibus hoc cunctis dixeris esse nouum.
        Heere lyes an honest lawyer, wot you what
        a thing for all the world to wonder at.
                  Made by Robert Wills 1632.

Edward Trelawny of Bake was the son and heir of Robert Trelawny,
and his wife Agnes Spry. He married Mary, daughter of Tristram
Arscott of Annery in Devon, and by her had one son and seven
daughters.[8] He is described by Richard Carew as " Master Edward
Trelawny, a gentleman qualified with many good parts."[9]

Bake lies about a mile and a half south-west from the church. A
carving of the Trelawny arms still remains at the present day farmhouse,
which stands a few yards back from the lane.

Cordelia Trelawny 1634

Arms: Argent, a chevron Sable between 3 oakleaves proper.

Position: Set into the wall under the window of the transept, or
Trelawny aisle.

Size: 6 feet by 2 feet 6 inches.

Condition: Good, except for the lettering which is almost obliterated.

Style: Within a border pattern of vine and roses is a cartouche
between two shields displaying the arms of Trelawny and Mohun.

Inscription: Here lyeth the Body of Cordelia Trelawny, third
    Daughter to Sr. John Trelawny, Knight and Baronett, who was
    Buried the 17th day of May, Anno Dommini, 1634.
    The Anagram { Cordelia Trelawnia
                { O,illa Credita wrnae
        O sad disaster! say, who can but mourne,
        To see so faire a flower clos'd in her urne;
        Yet reader pause awhile, and doe not call
        Griefe back, by thinking of her funerall.

[8] *Visitations C.*, p. 580.
[9] Carew, p. 117.

The slate bears the name of the carver—Anthonius Colly Fecit & Scul.[10]

Cordelia was one of the fourteen children (nine daughters and five sons) of Sir John Trelawny and his first wife, Elizabeth Mohun, of Trelawne.[11] She died at the age of fifteen. Her father was Sheriff in 1630 and a staunch Royalist.

Elizabeth Pope 1654

Position: Fixed to the wall at the west end of the north aisle.

Size: 3 feet by 2 feet.

Condition: Badly cracked and discoloured by heat, from the large stove which until recently stood beneath it.

Style: The epitaph and inscription are divided by a panel of incised strapwork which, with the lettering and verses, are all very simply wrought.

Inscription: Here lyeth the Body of Elizabeth Pope, the wife of
    Edward Pope, and their child, who were buried the 10th day of
    July Anno Domini 1654.

                    Maritus maestissimus

        Thy rest gives me a restless life
        Because thou wert a matchless wife;
        But yet I hope againe to see
        That day of Christ, & then see thee
        Methinks I heare a voice to crye
        oh come and taste! o come and trye
        those pleasures that are up on high
        above the starie spanglet skye
        O Man why wilt thou be so vaine
        thy noble spirit with sinne to staine
        and still neglect those future joyes
        for to imbrace poore present toyes
        Thy flowered youth and gallantrye
        must moulder in the earth away
        and then farewell all things I say
        none to a Saviour in that day.

    Those verses   ⎧ Now therefore wisedome get betime
    were of her owne   ⎨ live not so low but more sublime
    composing   ⎪ and heaven labor for to know
                        ⎩ before yt death doth strike ye blow.

---

[10] He also carved the Verman slate at Lamorran.
[11] *Visitations C.*, p. 577.

PERRANZABULOE
Perran and Elizabeth Hoskyn 1675 1677
(Plate 51)

Position: Attached to the wall of the south aisle. Originally in the old parish church which was overcome by sand and rebuilt in 1805 as it now stands at Lambourn.

Size: 5 feet 8 inches by 3 feet.

Condition: Excellent.

Style: Well carved in low relief, a border inscription surrounding two panels of flowers and an interesting epitaph.

Inscription: Here lyeth the Body of Perran Hoskyn Yeoman who departed this life in the Feare of God the 8th day of March Anno Dom. 1675. Here lyeth allso the body of Elizabeth Hoskyn his wife who was buried on the 18th day of July 1677
Whilst on Earth I Flourished like the Bay.
Much Earthly Comforts I inioy'd, but they
And all Physitians of no Value were
When in my way Death to me did appeare
Death did Arest me and would take no Baile
For to befriend me all Things here did Faile
Then Christ became my Friend and did deliver
My Soule from Death to Blessednesse forever.

Perran Hoskyn[1] lived at Trevithick, which lies less than a mile south from the old church in the sands.

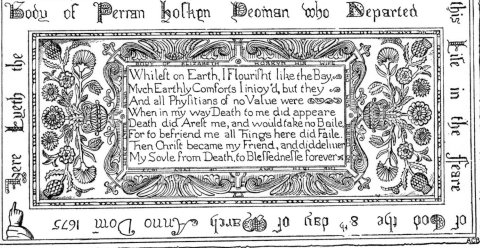

Slate Memorial in Perranzabuloe Church.

Cottey 1717—1769

Position: Attached to the wall of the south aisle.

Size: 5 feet by 3 feet 6 inches.

Condition: Excellent.

Style: Cut in low relief is a border design of thistles, roses, and a fruiting vine with two quaint little birds placed among the foliage. To these are added the inevitable emblems of death and mortality: a skull with crossed bones and an hour-glass. Inside the border an intricate floral pattern fills the top part of the tablet, and below it the inscription is set out on two arched panels. The small space which remained at the bottom of the slate has been filled with four more lines of inscription commemorating Edward and Christopher Cottey, the last men of their family. This slate was described by Dr. Dexter as having been formerly enclosed in a frame of coloured and moulded Renaissance plaster, portions of which were still attached when it was found, fixed to the north wall of the chancel, in the old Parish Church.[2]

Inscription:

Here
lieth waiting for
the resurrection of ye
just the Bodies of John
the Son of Edward
Cottey of this parish
Yeoman who departed
this life the 22 day of
July 1717 Aged 9 years
and of Ann his sister
who went to her ever
lasting rest August ye 5th
1713 Aged 4 months
The memory of ye
just is blessed prov the
10 7 verse

Here
also rests in Jesus
the bodies of Prudence
ye wife of Christopher
Cottey who departed
this life August the 9th
1718 Aged 32 years
here also rests with her
4 of her Children Ed-
ward aged 1 year 1714
and Edward aged 4
Years Anne aged 8
years & Elizabeth aged
3 years who all 3 depa-
rted this life in ye year
1720

Here Restth also in Jesus ye body of Mr Edward Cottey of Reen in this parrish who departed this life June 1725 aged 56
Here Restth also in Jesus ye body of mr Christopher Cottey of this parrish who departed ths life decr 23 1769 Ag 79

Edward Cottey was the only son of Christopher and Ann Cottey of Reen. He married Elizabeth Batten and had three children, Christopher, John and Ann.

Christopher Cottey, the only surviving child of Edward, married Prudence by whom he had Edward, Ann, Edward and Elizabeth. After the deaths of his wife and four children, Christopher married Elizabeth Tregian of St. Erme.

[1] J.R.I.C. Vol. XX, p. 473.
[2] J.R.I.C., Vol. XX, p. 473.

In his will dated 1724, Edward Cottey wrote "As I have no kindred save my son I bequeath Higher Reen and Angolla for the purpose of founding a Free school and maintenance of a schoolmaster for the poor children of the parish, should my issue become extinct."[3]

Reen is situated on high ground overlooking the sea and about $1\frac{1}{2}$ miles from the church. The Cottey family occupied the land from about 1615. Some evidence of the old house remains in the present-day farm, including a small granite doorway inscribed 1656 E.C.

POUGHILL

Laurence and Julian Braginton 1723 1739

(Plate 52)

Position: Inside the porch.

Size: 4 feet 10 inches by 2 feet 7 inches.

Condition: Fair.

Style: The slate is broken at the top, defacing some good carving of angels' heads. With the Latin inscription there is a stylised design of leaves, and a skull.

Below is a panel bearing the figure of a man carved in relief. He is shown in a reclining position, his head supported on his right hand and wearing a priest's cap and gown.

The figure is well carved and would seem to be a good likeness of the deceased; it is undoubtedly the work of Michael Chuke of Kilkhampton.[1] Unfortunately further damage to the slate has partly destroyed the carving. Laurence Braginton, who was vicar of Poughill, died in 1723 aged 72, and his wife in 1739, aged 85. He probably belonged to the Braginton family of Morwenstow, where the name Laurence is recorded in several generations.[2]

[3] Henderson, MSS, Vol. IV.
[1] See p. 173.
[2] F. C. Hamlyn, *History of Morwenstow*, 1930, p. 87.

K

Plate 52 POUGHILL
Laurence Braginton 1739

POUNDSTOCK

William and John Trebarfoote 1628 1630

(Plate 53)

Arms: Sable, a chevron between 3 bears feet erect and erased Or.

Position: Attached to the west wall of the nave, behind the font.

Size: 6 feet by 3 feet 3 inches.

Condition: Perfect.

Style: Handsomely carved in low relief are two semi-circular pediments elaborately patterned and supported by three fluted pilasters: above each is a charming angel's head. On the centre pillar is cut a shield displaying the arms of Trebarfoote, and fixed below it a small brass plate on which are some lines of a homespun verse. At the base is carved in relief, a curiously crude little male figure in Stuart dress, kneeling before a prayer stool and turning the pages of a book. A unique feature of the incised inscription is the carver's pretty capital letters, cut in relief.

Inscription: Heere lieth the body of William Trebarfoote Gent who was Buried the 24th Day of October In the yeere of our Lord 1628.

Heere lieth the Body of John the Sonne of William Trebarfoote Gent Who was Buried the 3 Day of May In the yeare of our Lord 1630.

Marie ye Wife of William Trebarfoote Gent was buried ye 2 Day of May Ano Dom 1616.

Aetatis suae 24 Ano Dni 1629
Soe soonest are the best flowers cropt yt hee
sawe soe much vertue as old age would see
but too fewe yeares God wott and was approvd
aged in good soe loving and belov'd
that of Trebarfoote may be truly said
the love of mankinde here lyes buried.

William Trebarfoote was the eldest of the five sons of John Trebarfoote and his wife, Margaret Penfound. He married Mary, daughter and co-heiress of John Babage of North Tawton, Devon, and had two sons and two daughters.

John Trebarfoote, son and heir of William, married Grace Dennis and had one daughter, Mary[1]

Trebarfoote lies a mile west from the church and some atmosphere of the old house remains in the present farm.

Visitations C., p. 455.

Plate 53 POUNDSTOCK
Carved figure from the panel to William and John Trebarfoote 1630

Charles Manaton 1732

Arms: Argent, on a bend Sable 3 mullets pierced of the first.

Position: In the churchyard near the south porch.

Size: 4 feet 10 inches by 2 feet 10 inches.

Condition: Very poor and almost covered with ivy and brambles.

Style: A ledger stone; within a border inscription is an epitaph and simple verse.

Inscription: Here lyeth the body of Charles Manaton of this parish, carver, and freeman of the city of London, who was buried the 20th day of June Anno Domini 1732: Aetat Suae 72.

The carving it hath been an art of old
And curiously was overlaid with gold;
As in the Ark and Solomon's Temple bright
With Cherubims most glorious to the sight;
So also it is useful in these later days,
Which did the intombed Artist's honour raise;
That after ages of his praise may sing,
And every Muse a wreath of Laurel bring,
To grace his brows for this most noble thing.
Now God is pleased to call me hence
I fly to him for my defence
I trust in Christ my Saviour sweet
Within his Arms to rest in sleep.

In his will Charles Manaton bequeathed to his godson, William Burgoyne of Trebarfoote, certain parcels of land called Juds Tenement in Tregolls in Poundstock parish. He also gave him " ten large glass buttons to weare upon a Coat in remembrance of me—." His nephew, Sampson Manaton of Stratton, he named as his heir and executor and gave specific directions in regard to a mortgage of £300 upon Trebarfoote.[2]

² C.R.O.

Remember
O man
thy ende

Plate 54 QUETHIOCK

Figured panel from the tomb of Hugh Vashmond 1599

QUETHIOCK

Hugh Vashmond 1599

(Plate 54)

Position: In the south-east corner of the north aisle.

Condition: Fair. Some damage to the pilasters and border pattern.

Style: On a plate, fixed to the wall and measuring 32 inches by 27 inches, is carved in low relief the figure of a man with a long spade beard wearing a doublet and trunk-hose and kneeling on a cushion. Before him, supported by an intricate pattern of strapwork, is an open book and behind him a skull: on a label above his head are the words " O Man Remember thy Ende." Underneath is fastened a long narrow panel 4 feet 10 inches by 1 foot 6 inches on which is inscribed the epitaph, between a rose and a fruiting oak tree with four of its fruits fallen. The top edge is decorated with the same simple border pattern and a pilaster at each end. A third panel, measuring 5 feet by 2 feet 2 inches, is cemented to a large " chest " of concrete. On this slate, which is rather worn in places, is a border inscription cut in a good decorative style and surrounding a centre design of strapwork, with a blank (or defaced) tablet and some lines in both Latin and English.

Inscription: Heere lyeth ye body of Hugh Vashmonde who had to wife Thomasien by whome he had 3 sonns and 4 daughters; he decessed ye 9th day of March 1599.

> My rase is runn, my goal obtainde,
> The combatt donn, the Conquest gainde.
> You that survive learne this of me,
> So runn, so strive, so Crowned be.
> Omnes una manet nox et calcanda semel via lethi
> H.G.V. Erected by Hugh Vashmond ye yonger 1607

In 1579, Hugh Vashmond, then aged about sixty, appeared before the court as a witness, to testify concerning the payment of tithe on land in the parish called Leighe.[1]

A farm called Trevashmond is situated about two miles east from the church, just over the boundary in Landrake parish.

---

[1] From information collected by the Revd. W. W. Willimott vicar of Quethiock, *circa* 1870.

Plate 55

St. Stephen-by-Saltash

Figured panel from the tomb of Frances and William Hechins 1593

ST. STEPHEN-BY-LAUNCESTON

John and Anne Bewes 1675

Position: Set against the north wall of the sanctuary.

Size: 6 feet by 3 feet 6 inches.

Condition: Very good.

Style: A handsome slate panel showing an elaborate design of two pilasters carved in low relief supporting a pediment of graceful patterns. The lettering of the inscription is most expertly cut and embellished with ornate capital letters.[1]

Inscription: In memory of Mr. John Bewes of Colacott in Woringiton who was here buryed on the Twentieseventh day of April in the year of our Lord God 1675 Atatis Sue 77
And also of Anne his wife she was buryed on the third day of May in the year of our Lord God 1675 Atatis 75

ST. STEPHEN-BY-SALTASH

Frances and William Hechins 1593

(Plates 55 and 56)

Arms: Argent, a cross patonce quarterly Gules and Azure, between 4 lions' heads erased Sable.

Position: At the east end of the north aisle.

Size: 12 feet 4 inches by 6 feet 8 inches.

Condition: Good.

Style: Carved in bold relief are three panels of slate, each set in a framework of decorated plasterwork, above a stone chest. The top panel displays a large shield and crest with the arms of Hechins impaling Denham. On the second panel is cut the figure of a man in full armour, kneeling on a cushion before a prayer stool with an open book. Behind him is his wife, also kneeling and wearing a plain full-skirted gown and a head-dress. Surrounding the two figures is a traditional design of scroll-work and supporting it the coarsely cut images of Adam and Eve. The bottom panel is of a hard black slate and expertly carved with an elaborate design of fruit, birds and putti, set round the kneeling figures of a woman with her five sons and five daughters. Some of the decoration has suffered from flaking. The top half of the woman's figure and nine of the children's faces have also flaked off. The inscription, now obliterated, was painted on the slate top of the stone chest. Attached to the wall at the east end of the monument is a slate panel bearing the arms of Wadham impaling Hechins. It seems likely enough that the panel displaying the eleven figures represents Dorothy (the only child of William and Frances Denham) and her family, and was formerly a separate monument.

[1] Several headstones in the churchyard are also decorated with very elaborate capital letters.

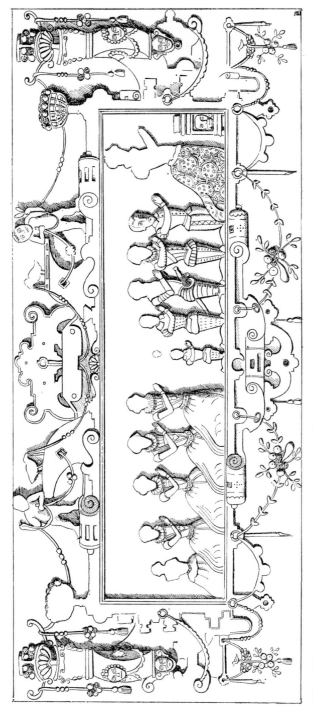

St. Stephen-by-Saltash

Figured panel from the tomb of William and Frances Hechins 1593

Plate 56

Inscription: Hitchins milde and Denham discreet
Conceiving longe a match full meete,
One daughter had, no children more,
Her God hath blest with issue store.
They gave her unto Wadham's worth;
their eyes sawe all her beautyes byrthe.
Then age prest on and ache withall
like busie stroakes before the fall—
And penn'd them in by Griefs constrayntes
untill at length to death they faynte.
Away drops first the lovely Henne,
the drooping Turtle followeth, when
With secret sighes, that love had taught,
sweet William for his Francis sought.
The faith of Christ each died in;—
Thus death doth end and life begin.

William Hechins (or Hichins) of Hole was the son and heir of William Hechins of Kenesbury near Saltash, by his first wife, Joan Peverell. He married Frances Denham of Wortham and by her had one daughter, Dorothy, who married George Wadham of Catherston in Dorset. Frances was buried 12th February 1593 and William on 11th December 1593.[1]

STOKE CLIMSLAND
Mary and Clare Manington 1605
(Plate 57)

Arms: Argent, on a bend Sable 3 mullets pierced of the first.

Position: Fixed high up on the wall of the north aisle, near the organ.[2]

Size: 3 feet 7 inches by 3 feet.

Condition: Good, except for the top and some of the border strapwork which has been lost.

Style: At the top of the panel are two large shields; one of eight quarterings including Manington and Hart; and the other of Manington impaling Hawkins of Tavistock. Between the shields is a branch of fruiting vine. Underneath is a Latin inscription and below it two ornamented pediments supported by three fluted pilasters, and further elaborated with two tiny figures holding hour-glasses and skulls; and a skeleton with two darts. Set in the two recesses are the figures of two young girls kneeling on cushions, the elder with an open book on a pedestal before her. Both girls wear little caps, ruffs and full-skirted gowns. At the bottom of the slate is an epitaph, also in Latin.

An interesting detail to be noted, in the fragment of decorated border, is the inclusion of a fleur-de-lis, a pierced mullet and three acorns; all repeated from the family arms.

[1] *Visitations C.,* p. 214.
[2] In 1820 C. S. Gilbert describes this and other monuments of the Manington family as " adjoining to the altar on the south side."

Plate 57   STOKE CLIMSLAND
              Clare and Mary Manington 1605

Inscription: Sampson et Judith Manington chariss filiabus suis
Clarae et Mariae aetate tenera morte a saeva ereptis Gementes
posuere
O pater, O mater, quid charae funera prolis lugetis cur sic
luminia vestra madent
Nunc nos aetherea dinum spatiamur in aula laudes et laeto,
fundimus ore, deo.

Mary and Clare Manington were the young daughters of Sampson
Manington and his wife Judith Hawkins. Mary died on the 4th of
December 1605 and her sister Clare died five weeks later, on the 11th
of January 1605/6.

(Plate 58)

Position: Cemented to the north wall behind the organ.

Size: 3 feet 9 inches by 2 feet 4 inches.

Style: Part of a slate slab bearing the kneeling figures of a man and
woman and two children, carved in relief. This slate has been badly
broken at the bottom, so that the carved legs of the boy and the lower
half of the girl's body are missing. The man wears a ruff and full
armour, and the woman is dressed in a full-skirted gown with a ruff and
traditional head-dress. The boy wears doublet and hose, and the girl
has a small cap and a chain over her bodice.

There is no inscription or shield of arms remaining by which to
identify this memorial. The date would probably be about 1600. As
this slate is very near to the Manington panel, it may be another of that
family, removed from the east end of the church.

STOKE CLIMSLAND

Plate 58

John Bagwell 1623

(*Plate 59*)

Arms: Paly, in chief a lion passant.

Position: Set in cement on the north wall near the organ and partly hidden by a large cupboard. This slate was originally on the north wall of the sanctuary.[3]

Size: 6 feet 2 inches by 2 feet 7 inches.

Condition: Good.

Style: Carved in low relief, within a border inscription, is the curious little bearded figure of a man kneeling on a cushion before a lectern bearing an open book. Behind him stands an awkward looking skeleton with a scythe, and in its left hand a big dart pointing into the man's back. The figures are surrounded by a pilastered arch ornamented with crude patterns and angel carvings: also these lines:

> I dread not death nor yet his dart
> for death itselfe is Kyllde
> By him that hath in every part
> the law for me fulfyllde.

Inscription: Here lyethe the boddy of the Worshipful John Bagwill, Batchelor in Divinity, Vicar of St. James and Kewbye, Rector of Stoke Climsland, Chaplain to His Majesty—Justice of the Peace & . . . 4th day of Maye, Anno Domini 1623.

> Master J. Bagwell being sicke made his epitaph.
> My byrthe plaice Exeter, my scholle I Oxforde call,
> My maintenance to live I find within Cornwall,
> I not without skill am, which I the preacher shew,
> That thou, O Cornwall! by these payn's may'st know
> This earth to me all curst, Heaven is my country too;
> This life I live is not true life another I pursue.
> O Christ to mee come thou, byd thou mee come to thee
> In earth my hope thou art, in Heaven my happiness shalt thou be.

There is a terrier for St. James and Keby (Cuby) of about 1602[4] in which John Bagwell asks for the Bishop's indulgence in respect of the information required concerning the vicarage, which, he explains, " . . . is not yet perfectly known to me as being very lately instituted and inducted thereto."

In 1614 he became also Rector of Stoke Climsland which was, like St. James and Keby, under royal patronage; and so continued as incumbent of both parishes until his death in 1623.

---

[3] In 1820 " to the left of altar."
[4] C.R.O.

Plate 59   STOKE CLIMSLAND
                            John Bagwell 1623

TALLAND

John Bevill 1579

(Plate 60)

Arms: Argent, a bull passant Gules armed and unguled Or.

Position: In the south-east corner of the south aisle.

Size: 4 feet 8 inches by 5 feet 9 inches.

Condition: Excellent.

Style: A magnificently carved tomb-chest. On the backplate, cut in relief, is an achievement of arms showing fifteen quarterings, set under a semi-circular pediment supported by two pilasters, each embellished with a figure; on the left a male and on the right a female. At the base is the family motto, " Futurum invisible " guarded by two praying demi-angels. On each side of this centrepiece is a panel bearing twelve lines of eulogizing verse. Above these panels are four shields of arms displaying the marriage alliances of four sons and four daughters, and a larger shield showing Bevill impaling Milliton.

On the top panel of the chest, set within a border inscription, is carved in bold relief the full-length figure of a man in a suit of elaborately patterned armour. He wears a long sword and a dagger and his head rests on his helm; nearby is a shield quartering Bevill and Bere. Between his feet is the figure of a bear and the letters J.B.

Along the top of the front panel is recorded the marriage alliance of each of the eight Bevill children. Below is a large incised shield and crest with animal supporters, showing Bevill quartering Bere and impaling Milliton. The panel is completed by two ornamented pilasters.

On the end panel are two more lines of inscription, and underneath, the large figure of " a bull passant " in very high relief. Along the edge of the top panel are the words, " Peter Crocker made this worke."[1]

Inscription: Here lyeth ye bodye of John Bevyll of Kyllygath Esquyre who deceassed the XXth of January beynge ye age of LXIII in anno Elizabeth Regine XXI 1579 he married Elizabeth Myllytun & had Issue by her lyvyng at hys deceaes 4 sonnes and 4 daughters.

> A Rubye Bull in perle Filde
> doth shewe by strength and hew
> A youthful wight, yet chaste and cleane
> to wedded feere most trew.
> From diamonde Beare inperle plot
> A leevinge hee achived;
> By stronge and steadfast constancy,
> in chastnes still contrived.

---

[1] Introduction, p. 3.

L

Plate 60   TALLAND
John Bevill 1579

To make all up a mach he made
with nature Millets, plaste
in nature seate; so nature hath
the former vertues graste
His Prince he served in good regard;
twyce Shereeve, and so just,
That justlye he still, on Justice seate,
three Princes hym dyd trust.
Such was his lyfe, and such his death
whose corps full low doth lye;
whilste Soule by Christe, to happy state,
with hym doth rest on hye.
Learne by his life such life to leade,
his death let platform bee
in life, to shun the cause of death,
that Christe may leeve in thee.

William Bevyll, Knight, eldest brother, he married Jane the
daughter of Thomas Arundell, Knight.
Peter Bevyll, second brother, married Grace, one of the
Coheyres of William vyell Esquier.
Phillipp Bevyll, third brother, married Elizabeth, daughter and
heyre of Anthonye Berrye Esquier.
John Bevyll, fourth brother, married Johan, the daughter of
Thomas Killyow Esquier.
Henry Meggs, Esquier, married Elizabeth, the eldest daughter
of John Bevyll Esquier.
Walter Kendall, Esquier, married Agnes Bevyll, the second
daughter of ye forsayed John.
William Pomeroye, Esquier, married Marye Bevyll, the third
daughter.
Humfrye Prideaux, Esquire, married Johan Bevyll, the fourth
daughter.
John Bevyll lyved yeares threescore three and then dyd yealde
to dye:
he dyd bequeath his soule to God, his corps herein to lye.
This Toumbe was made at the costs and charges of William
Bevill, Knight, Sonne and Heire of John Bevill Esquier, here
in toumbed, and the Lady Jane, wief unto the saied Syr William
Bevyll, Knight being the youngest daughter of syr thomas
Arrundell, Knight.

John Bevill was the son of Peter Bevill and his wife, Phillippa Beare.
He married Elizabeth, daughter of John Milliton of Pengersick Castle,
and by her had 4 sons and 4 daughters.[2] He was Sheriff of the County
in 1558 and a Justice of the Peace. In 1564 he was described as a

[2] *Visitations C.*, p. 31.

" very great enemy " to the reformed church,[3] but evidently in time became reconciled to the new order for he was again appointed Sheriff in 1575. In his will dated 19th January 1578/9,[4] the day before his death, he bequeathed to his youngest and unmarried daughter Joan her portion of £400, and the residue of his estate between his wife Elizabeth and eldest son William.

Killigarth stands on high ground about a mile west from the church. Richard Carew describing it in 1602, said, " Killigarth—hath lately foregone Sir William Bevill, whom it embraced as owner and inhabitant, by his sudden death, and is passed into the possession of the fair lady his widow, by her husband's conveyance. It yieldeth a large view of the south coast, and was itself, in Sir William's lifetime, much visited, through his frank invitings."

Although considerably altered and modernised, the old house is still apparent, well sited among its trees and pleasant grassland. It is now used as a country club and holiday centre.

Jane Mellow 1628

(Plate 61)

Position: Set in the floor before the chancel step.

Size: 6 feet by 2 feet.

Condition: Very good.

Style: This slate shows the incised figure of a woman in bed. Wearing a close-fitting cap and a small ruff to her gown, she rests against an embroidered bolster, wrapped in a blanket and holding her baby in her arms. Surrounding the figures is a carved post and part of the top or canopy of a four-poster bed. Below is a desk carved with a skull and bone and the words " Beehold you mee Such shall you bee." The epitaph is cut in a charming Elizabethan style of lettering.

Inscription: Joanna uxor Petri Mellow fuit Sepulta 20 die marty 1628 Heere lieth Jone Mellow and her little Sonne. Great traveill she indured by ye birth of him But beinge delivered GOD did soe decree That she and her sonne together shold dy Her body to the dust she did bequeath Her soule to GOD the same for to receive.

Feare not to dye   (Petrys   )
for soe must you   ⟨   ⟩ dixit
as well as I   (Mellow)

³ A. L. Rowse, *Tudor Cornwall*, p. 332.
⁴ P.C.C.

Ioanna
uxor Petri
Mellowfuit
Sepulta 20
die martij
1628

Bee
hold
you
mee

Such
shall
you
bee

Heere lieth Jone Mellow & her little Sonne
Greate traveil She indvred by ý birth of him
Bvt beinge delivered GOD did soe decree
That she and her sonne together shold dy
Her body to the dvste she did beqveath
Her sovle to GOD the same for to receive

Feare not to dye
for soe mvst yov
as well as I
} Petrvs
Mellow
} dixit

Plate 61 TALLAND
Jane Mellow 1628

ST. TEATH

Frances Bennet 1636

(Plate 62)

Position: Set against the west wall of the south aisle.

Size: 6 feet by 2 feet 6 inches.

Condition: Fair. Soft pale slate.

Style: Inside a border inscription, ornamented with fleur-de-lis and roses, is the full-length figure of Frances Bennet wearing a small-crowned hat and a cloak with her full-skirted gown. She holds a closed book in her right hand and a skull and bone in the other; behind her are the words Remember to Dye and the letters P.B. Below are the full-length figures of a small boy and girl named as John Bennet and Elyzebeth Bennet. The boy wears exaggerated falling sleeves to his long gown and the girl has a draped head-dress.

Inscription: Heere lyeth the Bodye of Franncis the wife of Phillipe
Bennet of this Parish who was Buried the XXX daye of October
Anno Domi 1636
      In life shee feared god
      In death shee showed ye same
      In life and death she did him praise
      And blest his holy name.

ST. TUDY

Humphry Nicoll 1597

(Plates 63 and 64)

Arms: Sable, a pheon Argent.

Position: Attached to the west wall near the font.

Size: 4 feet 6 inches by 3 feet, and 5 feet by 3 feet.

Condition: Excellent apart from some flaking on three figures.

Style: Carved in bold relief, on a panel which was evidently a back-plate, are the figures of Humphry Nicoll and his wife Jane, kneeling before a prayer stool on which is a closed book. The man is bearded and wears his hair long, with a ruff and suit of light armour; he also wears a thumb ring. The woman's face has flaked off but the shape of her head-dress and ruff remain. She wears a double chain and a cross with her traditional style gown.

Between the two figures is a shield of arms quartering Nicoll with Prideaux, Giffard and Trevenor. A second shield, showing Nicoll impaling Roscarrock, occupies the top left-hand corner and a helmet is carved in the opposite corner. Surrounding all is a mutilated border of scrollwork.

Plate 62 ST. TEATH
Frances Bennet 1636

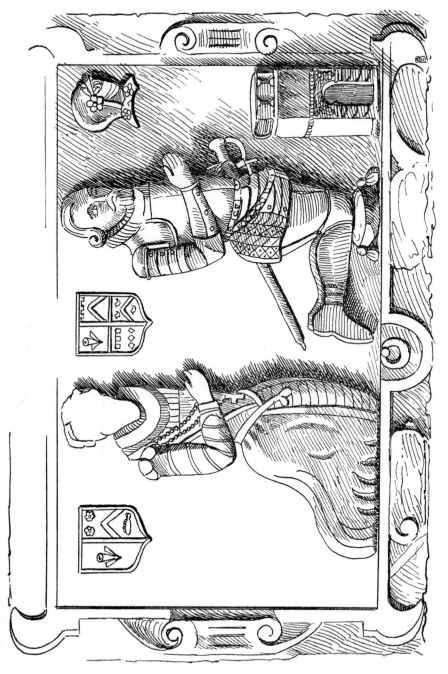

Plate 63

Sᴛ. Tᴜᴅʏ
Humphrey Nicoll 1597

The second, and front panel is more elaborate and shows under two pediments supported by decorated pilasters, the boldly carved figures of their son and heir Humphry Nicoll (with his wife Phillippa) and their four surviving daughters. The man, wearing his hair long, is dressed in a doublet and trunk-hose and kneels on a cushion; the upper part of his body has flaked off. His wife wears a head-dress and full-skirted gown with a decorated collar, necklace and chain; a bracelet and three rings. Above these figures are two shields displaying Nicoll quartering Giffard and Trevenor; and Nicoll impaling Rous.

The four daughters kneel beneath four shields of arms. The eldest, Mary, wears the traditional head-dress with a necklace inside her ruff and a patterned bodice and petticoat beneath her gown. The costume of the second daughter, Isabella, is similar but she does not wear a necklace. The third daughter, Jane, who was unmarried, wears a simple cap and gown with a high collar. Some flaking has occured on the upper part of the figure. The fourth daughter, Phillippa, wears a head-dress and gown like her elder married sisters except for a collar instead of a ruff, and all four sisters wear rings.

A slate plate bearing a shield of arms, now fixed to the wall of the south aisle, may have formerly surmounted the complete Nicoll tomb.[1]

Inscription: Hic Jacet corpus Humfridi Nicoll, armigeri, qui
  obijt vicesimo Sep—, 1597; aetatis suae sexagesimo secundo.
        Haec decoris monumenta tui nostriq. doloris
        qualiarung. tibi consecro (chare Pateris)
        Humfridus patrij Nicollas nominis haeres
        haeres virtutis qui cupio esse tuae
        Tu vitam moresq. mihi nomenq dedisti
        haec tibi quae potui marmora nuda dedi.
        Whoso with searchinge eye surveyest this stone
        and thinkst it marble, tis not so alone:
        It is a myrrour wherein thou mayst see
        both what yu shalt & what thou shouldest bee
        Say that thy line is ancient, so was his
        Whose part of earth to earth departed is
        What arms so ere thou bearest to blaze thy byrth
        at length yu must beare worms in field of earth.
        Add riches to thy gentry, all is one
        When the last houre approucheth both are gonne.
        An other must thy lands & lordships have
        and thou thyself be tenant to the grave.
        Say wisdome makes ye former couple three
        and thou enjoyest earths chief triplicity,—
        welth, worshippe, wisdome, he enjoyed them all
        whom yet this grave holds prisner, & yet shall

St. Tudy

Figured panel from the tomb of Humphrey Nicoll 1597

Plate 64

till the supremest Judg become his baile,
& quicken yt wch death hath causd to quaile:
with whome herein if yu wouldst have a part
As in the quailinge sure to have thou art,
make vertue then thy gentry, do not scorne
But count it thy best byrth to be new borne
good works thy chiefest welth, thy wisdom be'd
To know thy God, thyself, thy sinne, thyne end
So Nicoll livd, who holds this glasse to thee
To shew both what yu shalt & shouldest bee.

Humphry Nicoll of Penvose was the eldest son of John Nicoll and
his wife, Isabell Mohun. He married Jane, the eldest daughter of
Richard Roscarrock of Roscarrock (and widow of William Tremayne of
Upcott) and by her had one son and five daughters, one of whom,
named Isabell, died in 1570. His son and heir, Humphry, was M.P. for
Bodmin in 1627—1628. He married Phillippa, a daughter of Sir Anthony
Rous of St. Dominick by his second wife, and had six sons[2] and seven
daughters. He died in 1642 at the age of 65 and his wife died in 1668.

Mary, the eldest daughter of the first Humphry, was married in 1594
to Edward Lower of Tremeer in St. Tudy and had five sons and five
daughters. She died in 1626. Isabella, the second daughter, married
Robert Scawen of Molenick in St. Germans in 1599 and had six sons
and four daughters. Jane, the third daughter, died unmarried in 1607.
Phillippa, the youngest daughter, married Nicholas Godolphin of
Trewarveneth in Paul in 1599 and had two sons and five daughters.
She died in 1634.[3]

Penvose, set on the side of a delightfully wooded valley about two
miles north-west of the church, was the home of the Nicoll family from
1446 until 1721 when Joseph Nicoll sold the manor to John Hawke of
Liskeard.[4] " One of the finest of the hall screens stood, until a few
years ago, in the old mansion of the Nicoll family at Penvose, near
St. Tudy. Unfortunately this screen and other woodwork have been
sold to a purchaser outside Cornwall and the house itself pulled down
to make way for a modern farmhouse in which the charm and beauty
of the old mansion have not been reproduced."[5]

[2] Maclean, Vol. III, p. 367.
[3] Visitations C., p. 344.
[4] Maclean, Vol. III, p. 350.
[5] C.P.R.E. Cornwall Survey 1930, Henderson notes, p. 67.

ST. TUDY

Figured panel from the tomb of Alice Reskymer 1563

Plate 65

Alice Reskymer 1563

(Plate 65)

Arms: Argent, 3 bars Gules, in chief a wolf courant Azure.

Position: Under the west window of the north chancel aisle, now used as a vestry.

Size: 5 feet by 2 feet 9 inches.

Condition: Excellent, except for a slight flaking on two of the figures and some damage to the border.

Style: Magnificently carved in high relief, Alice Reskymer kneels before a prayer stool wearing the traditional head-dress and ruff, and a triple chain with pendant and matching belt over a richly patterned gown. Above her is a shield displaying Reskymer impaling Denzell. Behind the mother kneels her eldest daughter, Anne, dressed like her mother except that her gown is plain. Above her are two shields; the first showing Trelawny quartering Courtney; impaling Reskymer quarterly with Denzell, Treneweth and Skewys. The second shield displaying Mohun quartering Courtney; impaling the quarterly coat of Reskymer as before. The second daughter, Katharine, is dressed like her sister and there is above her a shield bearing the arms of Courtney, differenced with a label and crescent, quartering Tretherffe and Kemp and impaling Reskymer as before. The third figure is of Johanna, the youngest daughter, dressed like her sisters and with a shield above her showing the arms of Lower quartering Tresithney. Pentire and Upton impaling Reskymer as before.

A second panel (interrupted by a wooden door jamb) measuring 5 feet 4 inches by 2 feet 8 inches, bears a rather fulsome epitaph inside two borders of traditional pattern.

On another slab, which would have surmounted the original monument, is carved a lozenge displaying the arms of Denzell quartering Tresaster, Treneweth and Skewys. Surrounding the lozenge is a looped cord with tassels and two bows. This is a very curious display, for Alice Reskmyer was a widow and the use of bows, or knots of ribbon, was customary only for unmarried women; also the surrounding cord or cordeliere has been described as denoting a widow.

Note—An interesting disclaimer of this has been made by A. C. Fox-Davies.[6]

Inscription: Thryse blest and happye is the state
wherein the vertuous dye
Who live by death by making death
ther ladder to the skye
Who live in storyes, pictures, tombes
and monuments of brase

---

[6] A. C. Fox-Davies, *A Complete Guide to Heraldry*, p. 579.

Who live in offspringe and descent
all monuments that pase
Who lyve in lyving harts of frendes
and memoryes in shrynde;
Of those whose ever livinge love
can never dyinge find
So blest and happye is her state
who lyeth in tombed here
Whose soule ye heavens, whose corpes the earth;
whose love her frendes hold deare
Her byrth, her race, her lynnage & descent
howe well she lyvde, how happie she did dye
Thes scutchions blaze thes Images present
Thes tables teach, this hearse doth testifie
To all grave matrons which survive, set forth
Both to admyre and Imitate her woorth.

Alice Reskeymer was one of the daughters of John Denzell of Denzell near St. Columb, Sergeant-at-Law. She married William Reskymer, a Gentleman of the Chamber at the Court of Henry VIII, and the second son of John Reskymer of Merthen in Constantine, by whom she had four daughters.

John Skewys, uncle to Alice and step-father of William Reskymer, made them a gift of lands which included the manor of Polrode. This gift was later revoked, resulting in lawsuits. A settlement in favour of the Reskymers was eventually awarded to Alice after her husband's death and these lands were equally divided among their four daughters when the youngest came of age in 1570.[7]

In her will dated 7th January 1563 at Liskeard[8] a few days before her death, Alice Reskymer bequeathed " —to Anne Trelawny my eldest daughter my Sygnet ringe and a silver Cupp gilte. Item I give and bequeath to Fraunces my daughter my Wedding ringe. Item I give and bequeath to my daughter Jane my Turky ringe——." Her second daughter Katharine (named as sole executor) inherited land in Cornwall and Middlesex and the residue of her mother's jewels, plate and goods.

Anne, the eldest daughter, married John Trelawny, son and heir of John Trelawny of Menheniot, and in 1562 had two sons and one daughter. Her husband died in 1568 and she afterwards married Sir William Mohun by whom she had three sons and two daughters.

Katharine, the second daughter, married Peter Courtney, eldest son of Edward Courtney of Landrake, by whom she had five sons and three daughters.

Johanna, the youngest daughter, married Thomas Lower, son and heir of William Lower of St. Winnow, by whom she had six sons.

[7] C. Henderson, *History of Constantine*, 1937, p. 104.
[8] P.C.C.

The third daughter, Frances, died unmarried and before the monument to her mother was put up.[9]

Edward and Richard Billing 1621 1624

Arms: Or, on a bend Sable 3 bucks' heads erased of the first.

Position: Set in the floor of the south aisle.

Size: 5 feet 10 inches by 4 feet 6 inches.

Condition: Very worn.

Style: This slate is so badly worn that the carved figures are scarcely visible. However, on a bright day, it is possible to trace the kneeling figures of Richard Billing, holding a book in his right hand; and his wife wearing a hat with her full-skirted gown. Below them are the remains of eight shields and the figures of eight children.

The inscription, which is now quite worn away, was recorded by Sir John Maclean writing in 1879,[10] as follows: " Here Lyeth the Bodyes of Richard Billing Esquire, who died the 25th day of July anno (1624 and of Edward Billing his son who was buried) October anno 1621.

Richard Billing was the eldest son of William Billing of Hengar by his first wife, Elizabeth Babb. He married Elizabeth, a daughter of John Connock of St. Cleer, and by her had two sons and six daughters. He was Escheator and Feodary of Charles Duke of Cornwall and a man of considerable property with land in Michaelstow, St. Teath, Jacobstow, Warbstow, Advent and Lanteglos-by-Camelford.

In his will,[11] made a few days before his death at the age of fifty-four, he devised all his estate to his wife whom he described as a " loving and kind mother."

Edward Billing, the eldest son of Richard, pre-deceased his father and died unmarried at the age of twenty-three.

John, the second son, and heir, married Ann, daughter of Francis Trelawny of Plymouth in 1636. They had one daughter.

Jane, the eldest daughter of Richard, married John Killiowe of Lansallos in 1623. She bore 3 sons.

Philadelphia, the second daughter, was married in 1616 to Christopher Worthevale by whom she had one son and six daughters.

Margaret, the third daughter, married Oliver Hambly at St. Mabyn.

Grace, the fourth daughter, died unmarried in 1668.

Loveday, the fifth daughter, married William Hambly of Tregangeeves in 1639. She became a Quaker after her husband's death and suffered great persecution for her convictions.

The youngest daughter was named Phillippa.[12]

Hengar lies a mile north-east of the church surrounded by trees and thick shrubs. The present mansion succeeds the old one which was destroyed by fire about 1900.[13]

[9] Maclean, Vol. III, p. 321.
[10] Maclean, Vol. III, p. 325.
[11] C.R.O.
[12] Maclean, Vol. III, p. 365.
[13] L. V. Hodgkin, *A Quaker Saint of Cornwall*, p. 22.

WEEK ST. MARY
Humphrey Pethick 1663
(Plate 66)

Position: Set in the floor of the vestry, at the east end of the south aisle.

Size: 5 feet by 3 feet.

Condition: Excellent.

Style: Inside the border inscription is the incised figure of an angel in flight carrying a trumpet; cleverly drawn in an unbroken line of loops and coils.[1] Beside the carving are eleven lines of simple verse.

Inscription: Here Lyeth the Body of Humphrey Pethick of this Parish Who was Buried the 13th Day of October Anno Domini 1663.

> On whom ye ensueing Epitaph is made
> Mourn not for him that underneath doth lie
> Since tis decreed for all mankind to die
> His body here in sweet repose is layen
> Secure from sorrow trouble grief and pain
> No prisoner sigh no groaning of ye slave
> Disturbs the happy Quiet of his grave
> Sleep on my dear until ye day of doome
> Sleep on sweetheart until yr I do come
> I hope thy soul is gon to heavens high
> Lets all prepare to live eternally

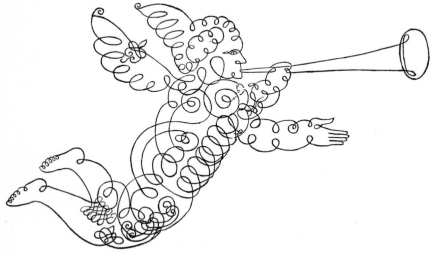

[1] Introduction, p. 7.

In his will dated 5th October 1663,[2] Humphrey Pethick names his wife, Prudence; a daughter Marie; brothers Thomas and Joseph; and sisters Marie, Ellnor and Emlyn. The name of Pethick still remains in the district.

Margery Gayer 1679

Arms: Ermine, a fleur-de-lis Sable, a chief Gules.

Position: Attached to the wall of the north chancel aisle.

Size: 5 feet by 3 feet 4 inches.

Condition: Excellent.

Style: A border inscription in good plain lettering, the first capital letter only being decorated, and with a pointing hand carved in the top-left corner. Inside the border are twelve lines of descriptive verse.

Inscription: Here lyeth the Body of Margery the wife of John Gayer of Whitestone, Gent, who was Buried the 28 day of February 1679.

> Since man's compar'd to an inverted tree,
> To this blest soule that name applied be.
> Sweet words, pure thoughts, good with her endear'd
> Her leaves, her Blossom, and her fruit appear'd.
> Her Pith was Vertue, Charity her Rinde;
> One verdant Branch from her is left behind.
> Death hath not cut her downe, who rather is
> To be a tree of life in Paradice.
> Short was her life, yet live's she ever,
> Few were her daies, yet dyes she never.
> She breath'd while, then went to rest,
> God takes them soonest whom he loveth best.

WERRINGTON

(Plate 67)

Position: Fixed outside, on the east wall of the church.

Size: 6 feet 6 inches by 3 feet 6 inches.

Condition: Fair, but weather-worn.

Style: Within a border of strapwork are carved in relief the kneeling figures of a man and woman and four boys. The man is bearded and wears a ruff with his doublet and trunk-hose; his hands and the hilt of his sword have flaked off. Before him is an ornamented prayer stool with a closed book upon it. Behind him is his wife wearing the traditional head-dress and gown of the period with a heart-shaped locket on a long chain. She also wears a ring on the first finger of her right hand. The

[1] C.R.O.

M

WERRINGTON

Plate 67

four sons, each kneeling like their father on a cushion, wear collars over their doublets, the eldest boy's with a lace edging. The hands and faces of the first, second and fourth boy have flaked off. It is of interest to note how only the figure of the woman faces full front.

This slate was undoubtedly part of a dismantled tomb that stood in the old church. Henderson says that the church was removed from within the park to its present site in 1740.[1]

The family commemorated is thought to be that of Drake. The barton of Werrington was formerly possessed by Sir Francis Drake (nephew of the Admiral) who sold it in 1651 to Sir William Morice.[2] Werrington Park lies less than a mile south of the Church.

WHITSTONE

Warwick and George Hele 1650 1652

Arms: Gules, a bend lozengy Ermine.

Position: Behind the altar frontal in the north chancel aisle.

Size: 6 feet by 2 feet 9 inches.

Condition: Excellent.

Style: Well carved in relief. Inside a border pattern are three semi-circular pediments supported on four fluted pilasters. The four spaces at the top are each filled with a delightfully carved angel's head. Under the first pediment is cut a small skull and the inscription with decorated capitals. The centre space is occupied by an achievement of arms with a shield showing Hele, father and son, quarterly impaling Ellacott and —. The third pediment surrounds the epitaph. This monument is very similar in design to that of Richard Spoure at Northill and is possibly the work of the same carver.

Inscription: Memento mori.

> Here lieth the body of George Hele, of Bennets, Esquire, who was buried the Xth day of March Anno Domini 1652. Here lieth also the body of Warwicke Hele Esq., his eldest sonne, who was buried the 4th day of January 1650.
>> Loe parts of nature rare,
>> Adornd with art;
>> Relations nere doe here
>> Conspire to part.
>> Imperious death projecting,
>> Ill can doe
>> That good which life
>> Could ne'er attain unto

---

[1] Henderson, *Cornish Church Guide*, p. 218.
[2] Lysons, *Devon*, p. 552.

Another:

Vita caduca vale, mihi mors tutissima merces;
Waile not your losse, ne blame my present fate,
Which steers me hence into a blisse-full state.
Wife, Children, friends, life, livelyhood, and all
Must then give place when God is pleas'd to call.
From this rich stemme a branch, whose glorious show
Transcends the shadowed face of things below.
Dull earth, too base his vertues to contayne
Yeelds foorth her dead, and life's restor'd agayne.
The cure's now wrought, The patient heald of payne;
Heale thus thy selfe And need no cure againe.

George Hele of Bennets was a younger son of Sir John Hele Sergeant-at-Law. He married Lucy, daughter of John Ellacott of Exeter and had four sons and three daughters. He was High Sheriff in 1628. Warwick, the eldest son of George, was married and had two sons. He died aged thirty-three.[1]

Bennets, now a large modern house, stands near the road, a quarter of a mile north-east of the church.

[1] *Visitations D.*, p. 464.

CARVERS

PETER CROCKER. Examples of his bold carving at Talland, Lansallos, St. Martin-by-Looe, Pelynt, and Duloe. 1579–1592.

ANTHONY COLLY. Signed his work "Anthonius Colly "; at Pelynt and Lamorran. 1634–1666. The gap of over thirty years between the two carvings is very apparent, in as much as one would scarcely credit them as the work of one man were it not for his signature.

ROBERT WILLS. He carved the decorated panel to Edward Trelawny at Pelynt 1632, and may have belonged to the family of Wills of Botus-fleming. A Robert Wills is recorded as brother of John, Vicar of Pelynt 1579–1629.[1]

MICHAEL CHUKE. Two examples of his carving in slate are at Kilk-hampton 1727, and Poughill 1739. He was the son of Stephen Chuke, a mason of Kilkhampton. His father sent him to London to learn his craft from Grinling Gibbons, the famous carver. He later returned to Kilkhampton where he married and had a family of five daughters.

In his will dated 1742[2] he gives " . . . unto my wife Elizabeth Chucke five pounds and I do also give her the Bed performed[3] the press and the Chest of Drawers in the fore Chamber and one Dousin of tin plates six pewter Dishes two pots a quilt and a white Diaper table Cloth and the little press bed and the easie Chair and the looking glass and the oaking table in the new room and two chairs and her Livering in the house one year after my death. Also I give unto my four Daughters Elizabeth Anne Julian and Mary to each of them fifty pounds apiece. Also all the rest of my Goods and Chattels not before mentioned and Given I do Give unto my five daughters Jane (Ellis) Elizabeth Anne Julian and Mary Chucke whom I do hereby make Executrixs Jointly of this my last will . . . unto my Brother Stephen Chucke twenty shillings and all my wearing apparrell . . . also I give unto my friend Thomas Crumb my cane and all my wiggs . . . " The inventory of his estate livestock and household goods amounted to nearly £600, quite a large sum for a man of his station, an indication that he was a clever and prosperous craftsman.

Of the monuments in Kilkhampton church, eight are attributed to the skill of Michael Chuke, and in the Churchwardens Accounts for the year 1724 there is an entry of £1 paid to Mr. Michael Chuke, for painting the pulpit and two pews. He became Churchwarden in 1727.[4]

In the churchyard, near the small door into the Grenville Chapel, is a simple weatherworn slate headstone which is inscribed:—

" Here lieth the Body of Mr. Michael Chuke of Heardacut in this Parish Carver who was buried ye 24th day of September Anno Dom 1742 Aetaus Sun 63 . . . "

---

[1] *Visitations C.*, p. 557.
[2] C.R.O.
[3] Furnished.
[4] W. Greener, *Kilkhampton Church*, p. 17—19.

JOHN BURT of Callington. He carved some charming panels and wall tablets, including the quaintly figured memorial to Ann Holliday at Callington 1753 and the finely lettered slate of William Saltern at Egloskerry 1742.

WILLIAM VAGUE who signed the fine slate panel commemorating John Silly 1672 in St. Minver church.

The names of many carvers of the eighteenth and nineteenth century headstones are known, as most of them signed their work.

In particular the name of Robert Oliver should be noticed, for the excellence of his lettering and the graceful proportions of his designs; in the churchyards of St. Issey, Ladock, St. Mawgan, Egloshayle and many others. The son of a carver he was born at St. Minver in 1798.

John Arthur of Egloshayle is another name to be found unobtrusively at the foot of many eighteenth and early nineteenth century stones. Arthur's style varied quite a lot so that his work is not easily recognised; but he produced some very original and sometimes amusing figures. A good example of his work can be seen on the headstone to the Martyn family (1790) which is preserved inside St. Columb Minor church.

In Mullion churchyard there are several headstones decorated with delicately cut figures of angels; one of these, carved by H. Skewes of St. Keverne in 1844, in memory of little Mary Skewes, is a delightful drawing of a female head.

During the early part of the nineteenth century there was a man living in Sancreed parish named Billy Foss, who was well known as a mender of clocks, a teller of drolls and for his skill as a carver of slate headstones.[5] The delicate precision of his carving and some of his quaint rhyming epitaphs can be seen in various churchyards in the Land's End area; such as Madron, St. Levan and Sennen. In the tower of Zennor church are two stones, and one of them in memory of Matthew Thomas, a miner, has some charming patterns and good figures cut on it.

Another interesting character was Daniel Gumb who besides acquiring a remarkable knowledge of mathematics and astronomy, also possessed a modest skill in the carving of headstones. He was born near Callington in 1703.[6] There is a slate stone against the east wall outside Linkinhorne church bearing his signature and commemorating Katharine Nicolls and Joan Mullis:—

" Here we lye without the wall
Twas full within they made a brawl
Here we lye no rent to pay
And yet we lye so warm as they."

Above this curious epitaph is cut, in relief, a skull and two skeletons one holding a scythe and hour-glass and the other a dart and spade.

[5] *Old Cornwall*, Vol. I, No. 10 p. 7.
[6] *Ibid*, Vol. II, No. 10, p. 1.

A man whose name will always be synonymous with slate carving in Cornwall was Nevil Northey Burnard, born, the son of a stonemason, at Altarnum.   One of his earliest carvings can be seen on a family headstone in that churchyard, where he carved, in relief, an eagle in flight against the sun's rays and signed it " N. N. Burnard Sculp aged 14." He later went to London through the generosity of Sir Charles Lemon M.P. and worked under Sir Francis Chantry R.A.   For some years he enjoyed great success as a fashionable sculptor but was eventually reduced to poverty through drink and returned to Cornwall to die in the Redruth workhouse in 1878.   For many years his pauper's grave was unknown in Camborne churchyard, until in 1954, through the efforts of some members of the Camborne Old Cornwall Society, it was found and a headstone of slate, given by the Delabole Slate Company, was set up.

ABBREVIATIONS

Carew	Richard Carew, *Survey of Cornwall* 1602 (ed. 1769).
C.R.O.	Cornwall County Record Office, Truro.
Collectanea	G. C. Boase, *Collectanea Cornubiensia*, Truro, 1890.
D. & C.N. & Q.	*Devon and Cornwall Notes and Queries.*
Esdaile	Katharine Esdaile, *English Church Monuments*, 1946.
C. S. Gilbert	C. S. Gilbert, *Historical Survey of Cornwall*, 1817–20.
Henderson	Henderson MSS. at County Museum, Truro.
A. J. Jewers	A. J. Jewers, *Heraldic Church Notes* (R.I.C.) 1882.
J.R.I.C.	*Journal of the Royal Institution of Cornwall.*
Lake	*Parochial History of Cornwall* (Published by W. Lake, 1867).
Maclean	Sir John Maclean, *History of Trigg Minor*, 1879.
J. H. Matthews	J. H. Matthews, *History of St. Ives*, London 1892.
P.C.C.	Prerogative Court of Canterbury.
Visitations C.	*Heralds Visitations of Cornwall* (J. L. Vivian) 1887.
Visitations D.	*Heralds Visitations of Devon* (J. L. Vivian) 1895.

GLOSSARY

Backplate: the panel behind and above a tomb.

Cartouche: tablet with an ornamental frame enclosing an inscription.

Ledger: a horizontal slab, covering a tomb or set in the floor.

Pediment: a small gable or circular ornament as used above a door.

Pilaster: a square column or pillar inserted partly in a wall.

Putti: small naked boys.

Strapwork: Sixteenth and seventeenth century decoration of interlaced bands similar to narrow strips of cut leather.

Tomb-chest: a chest made of slate or stone.

INDEX

179